Decorative Arts of Japan

工芸

Decorative

Arts of Japan

General Editor
CHISABUROH F. YAMADA

Associate Editor
ERIC SACKHEIM

Editors

Ceramics: FUJIO KOYAMA

Metal Work: OSAMU KURATA

Lacquer Ware: YUZURU OKADA

Textiles: TOMOYUKI YAMANOBE

Plate Captions Translated by
TOSHIZO IMAI and YUKO KOBAYASHI

講 談 社 Published by KODANSHA INTERNATIONAL LTD., Tokyo, Japan

Distributed by JAPAN PUBLICATIONS TRADING CO., Tokyo, Japan & Rutland, Vt.

Published by
Kodansha International Ltd.
with editorial offices at
3–19 Otowa-machi
Bunkyo-ku, Tokyo, Japan

Copyright in Japan, 1964
by Kodansha International, Ltd.

Library of Congress Catalog Card
Number 63–22011

First edition, 1964

Printed in Japan

the text and black-and-white prints by
Dainippon Printing Company, Tokyo

the color plates by Mitsumura Color Printing
Company, Tokyo; Benri-do Printing Company,
Kyoto; Hanshichi Photo Printing Company,
Tokyo; Choko-sha Printing Company, Tokyo

the binding by Wada Binding Company, Tokyo

Kodansha International books are distributed
outside of Japan by
Japan Publications Trading Co., Ltd.
C.P.O. Box 722, Tokyo, Japan
P. O. Box 469, Rutland, Vermont

Table of Contents

Preface

THE PRESENT volume is designed to present a historical survey of Japan's decorative arts through a series of full-color reproductions of carefully selected masterpieces. The term "decorative arts" is perhaps somewhat inaccurate, as the ceramic, lacquer, metal work, and textile objects dealt with in this book are all more appropriately considered objects of use than objects of decoration. The Japanese word is *kogei*, which might best be translated as "industrial arts," the connotations of which, however, would perhaps be even more misleading. So, following the lead of numerous Western museums, and for want of a better term, we have called our book *The Decorative Arts of Japan*.

Unlike the West, where these arts have been traditionally regarded as "minor," Japan generally considers her decorative arts as aesthetically on a par with painting and sculpture, and as decidedly "major." The four arts mentioned above are the main types of "major" art usually included under *kogei*. The Western reader may be surprised by the absence of furniture, which constitutes such an important part of European decorative art. The Japanese used comparatively little furniture in their households, and such specialists as the cabinet makers and joiners were almost non-existent; any artistic work done on furniture was usually the product of the artist in lacquer, especially *maki-e*, with which it was decorated (see Plates 60, 65, 70, 73, and 78). The glass industry, too, developed little in old Japan. One important branch of Japanese decorative art not represented here is the art of making beautiful decorated papers for writing, wrapping, etc., which, however, flourished as an art only during the Fujiwara Period, after which it is considered to have degenerated into a mere handicraft. (The decorative arts of modern Japan, and also the so-called folk-crafts, were not included as we felt they really required separate treatment if they were to be adequately covered.)

As for the selection of the plates, which of course constitute the heart of the book, pains were taken to include not only the representative masterpieces of each period, but also important works representing all the major phases in the historical development, as well as all the principal types of objects, of each of the four arts. In order to convey as accurately and as vividly as possible the aesthetic qualities of these works, we utilized the best available photographic and printing techniques and processes, and have presented all the objects in full color; the expense involved in this further limited the number of art works we could illustrate, but we believed that it was as important to do justice to the individual works of art as to the historical picture of these arts as a whole. We hope we have done both.

I am very grateful to the four experts, Mr. Fujio Koyama, Mr. Osamu Kurata, Mr. Yuzuru Okada, and Mr. Tomoyuki Yamanobe, each a leading authority in his field, who selected, in cooperation with myself, the pieces to be illustrated, and wrote the authoritative explanations for all the plates. These were translated by Mr. Toshizo Imai and Mrs. Yuko Kobayashi and then edited by Mr. Eric Sackheim.

As general editor and author of the introduction, I am deeply indebted to Mr. Sackheim for his help. He corrected my poor English and improved the clumsy style; in addition, I have found that Mr. Sackheim is not only a good writer, but also has a great knowledge of and good insight into Japanese art and culture. If my introduction is still clumsy in spots, it is undoubtedly because he tried to retain my personal, probably very Japanese, touch. I am grateful to the publisher for providing me with the opportunity of doing this interesting work; I only hope I have lived up to their expectations.

Thanks are also due to Mr. James Y. Kilpatrick and Mr. Masakazu Kuwata, who did the design, layout, and typography of the book.

Finally, I want, on behalf of the publisher, the various editors, and myself, to express our deepest gratitude to the owners and curators of the art objects illustrated in this book, for permitting us to take photographs of these precious, and often very fragile, objects (which in many cases are carefully treasured in storage) and to publish them. Thanks to their kindness and generosity, it has been possible for us to make color reproductions of many art treasures which have never before been published in color.

CHISABUROH F. YAMADA

Tokyo, September 1963

NOTE: In Japan, the family name precedes the given name, although it has become common to write the names in Western order when Romanized. In this book, when a person's name is written in the Japanese order, the family name is printed in small capitals.

Introduction

 ## THE BIRTH OF ART
(Jomon Period–late 3rd century B.C.)

Art germinated very early on the islands of Japan. The neolithic inhabitants of Japan, who lived primarily on fishing and hunting, began to make low-fired earthenware surprisingly early, more than seven thousand years B.C., according to recent studies based on carbon 14 radiation count. Yet they retained their primitive stage of culture a relatively long time: they did not have any proper agriculture to speak of,* did not learn the use of metal, and did not make any considerable development in the technique of their pottery (whose style, however, changed a great deal during this long period) until the third century B.C., when rice cultivation was introduced from the continent.

This long-lived neolithic Japanese culture is referred to as Jomon Culture because its pottery is characterized by *jomon* or "rope patterns" imprinted on the surface with ropes. A twisted rope or a stick entwined with a string or rope was rolled over the surface of the clay while it was still wet and soft, to imprint a pattern on the surface of the ware. Depending on the way the ropes were twisted or wound on the stick, innumerable variations in pattern were produced. The result was neither a rigidly geometric nor an arbitrarily free design, but rather a rugged, yet ordered, pattern. This method of decorating the surface seems to have originated in the eastern part of Japan and later to have spread throughout the country.

There were also other decoration techniques: designs imprinted with a shell, engraving with a knife, plastic decoration utilizing cords of clay, etc. In the middle and late Jomon Period, these were often combined with the rope designs which then served as a ground pattern or to give interesting texture to the surface.

The Jomon people were especially gifted with a vigorous and imaginative plastic sense, and their wares had from the beginning, remarkably powerful forms. Besides the pots and jars, they also made crude human figurines which have strong, expressionistic, almost demonic power, but they seem never to have attempted pictorial representation. Their gift for creation of three-dimensional forms is revealed most dramatically in their pottery, which was profusely decorated with fantastically shaped and modeled cords of clay; these pieces were made in the middle Jomon Period by the people who inhabited the mountainous region of central Japan and the area just to the east. Especially appealing are those with flamboyant cord decorations (Pl. 1). The spirit and energy of primitive man found unique, forceful expression in this flamboyant style in which the cords of clay struggle around

* Some scholars suspect the existence of some form of agriculture in the late Jomon Period.

the body, flame up above the edge, wind, swell, crush, and wave rhythmically, making this Jomon ware totally dissimilar to any other pottery the world has ever known.

This outburst of primitive artistic energy diminished gradually in the late Jomon Period, and the shapes of the vessels became more formalistic, though many different types of wares made their appearance.

 ## THE DAWN OF JAPANESE ART
(*Yayoi Period   late 3rd century B.C.–late 3rd century A.D.*)

The rice culture, which developed first in the western part of Japan (Kyushu) and gradually spread toward the east, brought about a new type of social life, a settled life based on agriculture. It is called the Yayoi Culture and lasted from the late third century B.C. down to the late third century A.D.*

The art produced by this new culture is entirely different in artistic conception from the Jomon pottery (except for some early and middle Yayoi ware from northeastern Japan). On the other hand, it already exhibits some of the characteristics typical of later Japanese art. Therefore, some scholars have suggested that the Jomon people were the aboriginal inhabitants of Japan, driven toward the east and then to the north by the ancestors of the present-day Japanese, who came to Japan in the third century B.C., bringing rice-culture with them from the continent. However, the most recent anthropological studies tend not to support this theory. Nevertheless, it is possible that a small group of people possessing the knowledge of rice-cultivation immigrated into Kyushu, perhaps from South Korea, acquired an influential position by virtue of their higher culture, and then somehow gradually mixed with the previous inhabitants of the Japanese islands, the creators of the Jomon culture. But it seems likely that changes in mode of life rather than racial differences were the main cause for the major transformation in artistic conception and expression.

Yayoi pottery is technically still quite primitive. Baked at low temperatures, lower than 900 degrees centigrade, these wares were not thrown on the wheel. But they are well-rounded, with sensitively curved surfaces. The plastic expressionism of the preceding period gives way to forms which are simple, serene, and stable. Yayoi ware is sparingly decorated, often not at all. When there are decorative patterns, they are geometric: simple, linear, and well ordered, but never rigid. These wares seem to reflect the placid, peaceful state of mind of a people who are content with their life and who are in harmony with the world in which they live (Pl. 2).

The Japanese learned the use of bronze and iron almost simultaneously from China, probably *via* South Korea. The metal products of this period include weapons, farming implements, mirrors, etc. They are mostly made in imitation of Chinese originals. Peculiar to Japan, and artistically the most interesting are the *dotaku*, more than three hundred of which have been excavated. These *dotaku* are large, hollow, cast bronze objects which look like slightly flattened bells (Pl. 30 and 31). It is believed

* The Jomon style survived much longer in the east than in the west, as the Yayoi Culture spread gradually from west to east. Some elements of Jomon style remained even in the Yayoi pottery of the middle period in the northeastern part of Japan.

that they were originally modeled after small Korean bells, and were probably themselves used as bells at the beginning; but they seem later to have acquired some symbolic significance and to have been put to ritual use. At any rate, they became larger in size and more elaborate in workmanship in the latter half of the Yayoi Period. Japanese metal artists of the time must have devoted the best of their skill to the *dotaku*. They were apparently used in the Kinki district and adjoining areas; that is, in that part of Japan where a little later the ancestors of the Imperial Family established their first state.

They are decorated with simple geometric designs cast in relief, one of the most common designs being the so-called "running water pattern" which is basically a number of parallel lines running back and forth in successive U-turns (Pl. 30). It is a purely abstract pattern, but, whereas the representational intent should not be made too much of, it is not impossible that the abstraction was actually based on the reduction of the visual impression of running water to its geometric essentials. Thus it is of interest, and perhaps of some significance, that running water and waves similarly abstracted to their elements—rhythmically winding parallel lines—later became one of the favorite motifs of both Japanese painting and decoration.

Some *dotaku* bear simple pictorial representations (Pl. 31), which do not show any continental influence, depicting various subject matter in bare outlines, either in profile or front view (and occasionally as seen from the top). It is a naive "conceptual art," in which respect it does not differ much from primitive arts elsewhere; but it does differ in other respects. There is no intentional distortion, nor is there any effort on the part of the artists to fill up all available space as there is on the part of most primitive artists. The artists of the *dotaku* represented only one, or at most a few objects suspended in the space defined by each separate section. The subject matter includes animals, birds, tortoises, and men engaged in various daily occupations such as hunting, pounding rice, etc. These are all represented in simple outlines, but with such obvious affection that even a wild boar to be hunted is rendered with considerable charm (represented on the other side of the illustrated *dotaku*).

If the Yayoi people regarded nature with awe (and the origin of Shinto was nature worship), it was with love rather than fear. This love of nature, becoming more profound as time went on, remained one of the primary creative forces in Japanese art, including the applied arts, throughout its history down to recent times. And the preference for simplicity which we have noted in the applied art of this period also retained its hold on the aesthetic consciousness of the Japanese people.

 THE AGE OF MONUMENTAL SEPULCHERS
(Kofun or Tumulus Period   late 3rd century–537)

In the late Yayoi Period, that is, during the second and third centuries of the Christian Era, Japan was divided into scores of small clan-states. One powerful clan which was ruling in the Yamato Plain around Nara emerged as a dominant force in the following century, and finally won suzerainty over the other clans in central and western Japan. This was the beginning of the Japanese State (with the ancestors of Japan's Imperial Family at its head), which gradually expanded its territory eastward and westward. The early period of this Japanese State is usually called the Tumulus Period because of the burial custom among the powerful clans of building monumental sepulchral mounds for their chiefs.

By now Japan had developed a closer relationship with Korea, and her culture and economy had advanced considerably. Those at the Imperial Court, as well as the chiefs of other clans, could afford not only to import applied art objects from the continent, but also to maintain craftsmen, both immigrant and native, for the production of luxury items. Techniques in various fields of applied art advanced rapidly during the fifth and sixth centuries.

In pottery, the Yayoi type of ware was still produced everywhere. Only in the use of finer clay and in the limited utilization of the potter's wheel can we recognize some technical development. In the fifth century, probably in its latter half, another, technically more advanced pottery type was introduced from Korea; the new pottery was called Sue ware. This ware was thrown on the wheel and fired in a kiln at a high temperature, more than 1100 degrees centigrade. As would be expected, the early Sue ware aesthetically shows a strong Korean influence. But this type of pottery eventually became entirely Japanized and continued to be produced in Japan down to the thirteenth century. We reproduce here one Sue piece from the Nara Period (Pl. 3).

The most representative art objects of this age, of course, are the *haniwa*, especially those representing human figures, birds, and animals. However, as this cannot really be called applied art, such clay sculpture does not fall within the province of the present book. To illustrate the period, we have chosen for our plates three interesting pieces of metal work, two mirrors and one helmet (Pl. 32, 33, and 34). Mirrors possessed both religious and political significance. Those shown here represent two different styles, one imitating Chinese models, the other decorated with original designs indigenous to Japan. The strange animal motifs in Plate 32 are of the former type: in its workmanship and in the excellent quality of the metal (whitish bronze) the mirror demonstrates the considerable heights of which Japanese craftsmen were technically capable at the time; but in design it is purely imitative. On the other hand, the design of the mirror in Plate 33, abstract, and so geometric that it could be made solely by the use of compasses, reveals the native Japanese penchant for simple, clean-cut design.

Another of the characteristics of Japanese decorative art is its strong preference for naturalistic design: subjectivistic, forced stylization of natural forms is avoided and an attempt is usually made to retain the intuitively apprehended forms of nature in decorative design. However, any act of transforming the perceived beauty of nature into art requires an aesthetic sense of abstract form on the part of the artist; without it, there can be neither good painting nor good decorative art. The Japanese artists of this as of other periods had the requisite sense of design, which was directed especially toward tidy, well-balanced, clear-cut designs. This principle underlies the naturalistic motifs of most Japanese decorative art, but rarely reveals itself so obviously and directly as in the geometric design of this mirror. Another masterpiece in which the same principle is apparent is the celebrated architectural design of the Ise Shrine, which basically dates from this era.

In the latter half of the period, work in gold and silver was begun, and gilt bronze became a favorite material for luxurious metal work, much of which was in imitation of Chinese or Korean originals. The illustrated helmet (Pl. 34) presents a good example of a design which is not a mere Chinese imitation.

12

First Period of Chinese Style

(Suiko and Hakuho Periods 538–709)

The custom of building monumental sepulchers lasted until the seventh century. But in the central part of Japan, primarily in the Yamato Plain, an entirely new phase of civilization was inaugurated during the second half of the sixth century in consequence of the self-conscious and vigorous introduction of Chinese culture, and particularly of Buddhism, which was officially introduced to Japan, according to recent studies, in 538 A.D., but began to flourish only in the last quarter of the sixth century. The Japanese people of this region had apparently attained a cultural level which gave them both the capacity and the will to learn and absorb cultural influences from the much older, already mature civilization on the continent.

Much of Chinese art was introduced to Japan, mostly by way of Korea, in connection with the new religion—for building and embellishing Buddhist temples, for making Buddhist images and adorning them, and for furnishing the necessary implements needed to perform elaborate religious rituals. The first great protector and propagator of Buddhism in Japan was Prince Shotoku, an unusually gifted individual, both in learning and politics, who was prince regent for the Empress Suiko (reigned 592–628 A.D.). Under his tutelage, Buddhist art in Chinese style took firm root in Japan. Many of the architects and craftsmen were either Chinese or Korean immigrants or their descendants, but the Japanese art of this so-called "Suiko Period" reflects, not the contemporaneous art of China, but rather the Northern Wei style of the early sixth century, or, in some cases, the style of a slightly later period. Although we still have a considerable number of pieces of sculpture from this era, very little remains of the applied arts.

The set of eight gilt bronze plate hangings with designs of flying heavenly beings in openwork in Plate 35 were probably made in Japan in the first half of the seventh century, and are good examples of the metal work of the period: it is obvious that a new element of grace has entered Japanese applied art. The tendrils rendered on both sides are a Chinese variation of the honey-suckle motif which came from Greece *via* Persia and Central Asia.

The two pieces of textile fabric reproduced in Plates 83 and 84, one a kind of ikat weave and the other a brocade, are said to have been used by Prince Shotoku. They are considered to have been imported from abroad, but the latter might conceivably have been made in Japan. We have illustrated them, though, primarily to show what kinds of textiles were imported and actually used at this time, and what sorts of models were available to Japanese craftsmen, as well as to indicate the extent of Japan's cultural contacts with the world at large, indirect though they may have been.

An important textile piece of this period, the Japanese origin of which there is no doubt, is a large pictorial representation in embroidery of the Buddhist Paradise, a few fragments of which are still preserved in the Chuguji nunnery near Nara. As these fragments are too scanty to indicate the splendor of the whole piece, we are not illustrating them in this book, although they constitute valuable materials for the study of both the painting and applied art of the period.

This wall hanging is interesting in another respect: it gives us important information regarding the spiritual background of the art of the age. The text, which was inscribed in embroidery, is recorded in an early book, the *Jogu Shotoku Hoo Teisetsu*, and quotes the following words of Prince Shotoku to his Princess Consort: "The world is vanity; only the Buddha is real."* This view of life and the world, and the concept of an abstract absolute existence, such as that of the Buddha, in contrast to the world perceived *via* the five senses, must have seemed unusual to the Japanese, who had been worshiping nature with a naive simplicity and had not hitherto expressed any serious doubts about the life they lived. At that time, there obviously could not yet have been many who had such a profound grasp of Buddhist teachings as did Prince Shotoku. Nevertheless, an important beginning had been made, which ultimately led the Japanese to view the world and life from an entirely new point of view, and helped considerably to elevate the spiritual life of Japan.

Of course it was not only Buddhist influence which broadened and deepened Japanese sensibilities at this time (actually the really strong Buddhist influence on Japanese thought came much later). Chinese literature must also have contributed a great deal. And, most important of all, life itself became more complex, which undoubtedly encouraged a more reflective attitude on the part of the Japanese. The beauty of Chinese art, too, taught the Japanese how to appreciate the beauties of nature more profoundly, and, at the same time, contributed to a more refined sense of form and color.

From the continental art, many new elements were ingested: not only new materials and techniques, but also new motifs and conventions. Such technical acquisitions alone, however, might merely have led to poor, uninteresting, imitative works; were it not for the spiritual growth which took place at the same time, the Japanese would not have been able to create such masterpieces of sculpture as, say, the Shaka Triad by Tori in the Horyuji monastery** or the Kudara Kannon, also in that monastery. The same thing can be said of the decorative arts of this period; and the new grace has already been noted in connection with the metal plate hangings.

In the following Hakuho Period (645–709 A.D.) art became still more graceful under the influence of the Chinese art of the Sui and early T'ang Dynasties. The decorative art of this period, too, exhibits a more mature, refined sense of form. The beautiful reliquary set found underneath the pagoda of the Shufukuji monastery (Pl. 36) is a good example of the decorative taste of the time. None of the boxes of the set have decorative designs on the surface; rather, they demonstrate the beauty of the material itself and of the pure form. The corners of the boxes are gracefully curved, though the four edges of each lid are not curved but slanted. This form gives a slight sense of volume which, however, does not approach the rich mass of the boxes with curved-edged lids and amply curved receptacles, made in the following Nara Period (Pl. 37 and 38).

---

* We can find similar Buddhist ideas in the commentary and explanation which Prince Shotoku is supposed to have written on three Buddhist sutras. But there is some doubt as to whether the book was actually written by the prince.
** Though the word "monastery" might not always seem quite appropriate, we have used it to distinguish the temple complexes, containing many buildings, from the individual structures within them.

SECOND PERIOD OF CHINESE STYLE
(Nara Period 710–793)

During the preceding period, the Japanese Imperial Court had remodeled its government after the strongly centralized state of T'ang Dynasty China, had begun to imitate Chinese court protocol, and had finally started to copy the palace and city plan of the Chinese capital. In 710 A.D. they set up in Nara a new capital city modeled after Ch'ang-an, the great metropolis of T'ang, though naturally on a considerably reduced scale. This was the beginning of the Nara Period (710–793 A.D.) which lasted until a new capital was set up in Kyoto in 794 A.D. It was a period when the highly developed, cosmopolitan Chinese culture of T'ang China exercised an overwhelming influence on Japan, especially on court aristocratic and Buddhist circles. The luxurious Chinese-style decorative art flourished, as the demand for it was strong, both from the Imperial Court and the Buddhist monasteries, which prospered even more than before under the sponsorship of the emperors, who regarded Buddhism as a religion ideally suited to protect the state and bring good fortune.

Japanese craftsmen of this period, many of whom were the descendants of immigrants from the continent, mastered the techniques and conventions, as well as the more subtle intellectual, emotional, and aesthetic content, of T'ang decorative art so well that it is very often difficult to distinguish the Japanese works from their Chinese models. Today Japan still boasts countless extant examples of the decorative art of this period. The Shosoin Repository in Nara is literally a treasure house of such works. The catalogue contains more than 3000 entries (the number of separate pieces would amount to a considerably higher figure) of decorative art (and other) objects from eighth century China and Japan, or in some cases even from Sassanian Iran, and preserved almost intact from the Nara Period to the present (Pl. 5, 39, and 57). The nucleus of this treasure consists of personal belongings of the Emperor Shomu, dedicated after his death to the Great Buddha of the Todaiji monastery in Nara in 756 A.D. There are objects of virtu, mirrors, stationery articles, musical instruments, screens, priests' robes, arms, armor, and many other things, all exhibiting the most elaborate workmanship in a variety of techniques and materials, including ivory, gold, silver, mother-of-pearl, amber, glass, lacquer, etc.

They are sumptuous, luxurious articles, beautifully designed in the opulent T'ang Dynasty style and often richly decorated with stylized floral, bird, animal, and human figure designs. Essential for the study of Chinese art, these pieces are also important for the study of the applied art of Nara Japan. However, they are so Chinese in taste and style that in many cases we cannot be sure whether the workmanship is Chinese or Japanese—and the same might be said of other decorative art objects of this period preserved elsewhere. Therefore, in spite of the splendor of Nara decorative arts, we have illustrated rather few examples (Pl. 3–5, 37–39, 57, and 83)—eight in all—as our emphasis in this volume is always on the specifically Japanese qualities and characteristics of the arts presented. This paucity of illustrations should by no means be taken as a denial of the importance of the part played by this period in the further development of Japanese decorative art; what the Japanese of that age learned from China became one of the primary sources of visual language and technique for the decorative art of all the periods to follow.

The eight items illustrated are either pieces whose Japanese origin can be definitely proved or works which most experts consider to be Japanese. The Sue bowl (Pl. 3) technically derives from the Sue pottery of the Tumulus Period, but its amply curved, powerful form shows the strong influence of T'ang Dynasty style prevalent in the Nara Period. This piece is coated with an attractively streaked natural ash-glaze; the intentional application of glaze started in Japan only with the Nara imitation of the Chinese so-called "three-color" ware (Pl. 4 and 5).

In the Shosoin there are thousands of pieces of textile, illustrating various kinds of weave. Some have woven designs, some dyed designs. In addition to the simple technique of stencil dyeing, three more elaborate techniques were also used for dyeing designs on cloth: the tie-and-dye technique (*kokechi*), a variety of batik work utilizing wax (*rokechi*), and a kind of stencil dyeing whose principle was to put a piece of cloth folded in two between two wooden boards with openwork designs through which the dye was applied. This third method could produce cloth dyed with multi-colored designs, but the details of the technique are not known today as it has not been used since the Nara Period. The illustrated piece of fine, green gauze (Pl. 82) with a woven design of small flowers, bears in addition another design of large flowers dyed in this *kyokechi* technique. It is noteworthy that not only this technique, but also the technique of wax-resist dyeing went out of use in the next period, when the more purely national culture began to expand and develop, while the tie-and-dye technique was continued and improved, eventually leading to the gorgeous, distinctly Japanese, effects of the beautiful *kimono* materials seen in Plates 89, 90, 92, 93, 94, 95 and 96. The use of wax might have declined in popularity because of a shortage of wax, but there could also have been some purely aesthetic reasons for the decline of both of these methods: the effects they produced might not have coincided with the artistic intentions of the Japanese artists who had begun to develop their own national taste.

 THE GRADUAL GROWTH OF NATIONAL CULTURE
(Jogan Period 794–893)

In 794 A.D. the capital was moved to Kyoto, then called Heian-Kyo. Again the city was laid out after a Chinese model. But in the architecture of the Emperor's palace there were many Japanese innovations in accordance with national custom and taste. For instance, the wood, the main construction material, was no longer painted as it was in the previous period, but was left plain so that the beauty and natural quality of the material itself were revealed. The building was not constructed on a stylobate, or high stone base, which separated the building from the ground and from its surroundings as in the case of Chinese architecture; but the floor was built high on posts erected at ground level, thereby reviving an old Tumulus Period tradition.

During the first century after the establishment of the new capital, called the Jogan Period (794–893 A.D.) in art history, the imported Chinese culture was gradually nationalized, but the prestige of things Chinese still remained high, and learning from China continued. The Chinese centralized government system too was kept, although it had already begun to disintegrate from within, as the influential court aristocrats, who were at the same time high government officials, disturbed the system by trying to acquire for themselves tax-free, independent manors. However, the Japanese had by then learned enough from China to be ready to develop their own culture, and they became more and more aware of various differences between the two nations in many different spheres.

One conspicuous example of this nationalization, or growth of the native culture, was the development of the Japanese syllabary, called *kana*, which was accomplished by using certain Chinese characters in abbreviated form as phonetic symbols. This phonetic writing system was gradually developed and perfected during the ninth century. In painting, however, the T'ang style was faithfully followed. Even the subject matter of the secular painting was Chinese, at least during the first half of the century. But in the latter half the Japanese started to paint, as contemporary literature tells us (for no work of secular painting has survived from this period), Japanese themes including intimate Japanese landscapes. As one would expect, this tendency led to a gradual nationalization of style, the process being completed during the following Fujiwara Period.

In the field of applied art, too, we can observe the growth of national culture in the development of the new technique of gold and silver lacquer decoration called *maki-e*. By the masterful application of this technique the Japanese developed, in the next and later periods, the splendid national art of lacquer—for the history of Japanese lacquer art is virtually the history of *maki-e*.

The art of true lacquer, made from the sap of a tree (*Rhus Vernicifera*) containing urushiol, is a speciality of the Far East. The Japanese were using lacquer quite early, in the late Jomon Period. But the Chinese had developed this art so early that they could already produce wares painted richly with polychrome lacquer in the third century B.C. They later developed other elaborate techniques, including painting with a mixture of gold dust, glue, and water, for embellishing their lacquer wares.

It is still problematical whether the technique of *maki-e* originated in China or Japan, but it seems fairly safe to assume that it was invented in Japan since no example has been found in China to date, and there does not appear to be the slightest reference to it in old Chinese literature.

Maki-e, which means literally "sprinkled picture," is a special type of lacquer decoration, usually in gold or silver, whereby a design is first painted with slightly colored lacquer, either on a finished lacquered surface or on a simple, natural ground, and, while the lacquer is still moist and sticky, dust of gold or some other metal is sprinkled over the design so that the fine powder sticks to the painted part. After the painted lacquer is dried, the metal powder which may have adhered to parts of the surface other than the design itself can easily be dusted off. The design, or sometimes the whole surface, is then coated once more with colorless lacquer and polished, thus bringing out the brilliance of the metal. Depending upon the quality of the metal and the fineness of the dust, as well as on whether it is sprinkled thickly or sparsely, a variety of textural effects can be achieved. Sometimes the result looks like an inlay of cut gold plate, at other times like a painting in gold.

There are many sumptuous lacquered objects in the Shosoin. They are often richly decorated with designs done in inlay of gold, silver, mother-of-pearl, amber, ivory, etc. Some pieces bear designs painted in gold and silver dust mixed with water and glue, which incidentally can easily be worn off and does not exhibit the brilliance of the metal. But in the whole Shosoin there is only one lacquered object, decorated with a tendril-like design, which is executed in what seems to be a primitive form of *maki-e*: the object is the lacquered scabbard of a sword. In the original inventory of the dedicated treasures it is described as a scabbard done in *makkinro*, a term which to date has not been found in any other ancient document or book, Chinese or Japanese. This *makkinro* might well have been the origin of the *maki-e* which was to be gradually perfected during the ninth century. The word *maki-e* appears for the first time in the *Taketori Monogatari*, a Japanese tale written sometime around the middle of the century. The only extant specimen of *maki-e* decoration which seems to date from this century is an arm-rest now in the Fujita Museum in Osaka. The earliest piece with *maki-e* decoration whose date of manufacture can be documented (919 A.D.) is a lacquered box, decorated with floral arabesques and *kalavinka* birds in gold and silver *maki-e*, owned by the Ninnaji monastery in Kyoto.

But before we proceed to the next period, we should say something of the esoteric Buddhism introduced into Japan in the early ninth century by the great priest Kukai who established the Shingon sect in Japan, and also by another priest, Saicho who, by adapting the Shingon ritualism started a Japanese version of the Tendai (T'ien-tai) sect based on the *Pundarika Sutra*. These two new sects flourished through this and the following Fujiwara Period, and profoundly influenced the art of the age. They liberated Japanese Buddhism from the worldly union with the state in which it had become involved during the Nara Period. Furthermore, they did a great deal to instruct the Japanese in Buddhist teachings, and thereby turned Japanese aesthetic consciousness toward the transitory nature of the world, an attitude which pervades the literature of the Fujiwara as well as later periods. On the other hand, it is also true that these two esoteric sects gradually degenerated into a mere magical ritualism, employed for the purpose of ensuring happiness and warding off evil for the personal benefit of the court aristocracy. At any rate, since the rituals required implements of various strictly prescribed shapes, such as the *vajra*, or *vajra* bell, Japanese craftsmen found another outlet for their genius in this kind of Buddhist art, all the more so as the wealthy aristocracy sought to endow the rituals with as much artistic embellishment as possible. A set of such ritual implements owned by the Itsukushima Shrine near Hiroshima, probably made in the early thirteenth century, is illustrated in Plate 46.

AGE OF COURTLY ART
(Fujiwara Period 894–1184)

In the year 894 A.D., SUGAWARA Michizane, a minister and distinguished scholar, was appointed official envoy to the Chinese court of the T'ang. But he advised the emperor that it was useless to send an embassy to the T'ang government, whose political power was decaying, and his advice was accepted; from that time, Japan suspended official intercourse with China for about three hundred years, during which period she also did not have any diplomatic relations with Korea, although there was some private trading and communication with the continent. Actually no embassy had been sent to the Chinese court since 838 A.D., but this incident of 894 indicates the change in the Japanese attitude toward China; therefore the date is usually used in the history of Japan to mark the beginning of the Fujiwara Period, the age which saw the creation of a new, distinctively national culture.

Less than a decade after this incident, Michizane was driven out of the court by a political intrigue involving the Fujiwara family, which was trying to establish its absolute power over the government. Michizane was the last obstacle in their way, and for about two and a half centuries an aristocratic culture flourished, with the Imperial Court as its center, under the supremacy of the Fujiwara clan.

The courtiers, especially the members of the Fujiwara clan, indulged in an elegant and luxurious life, relying on the great wealth they derived from their numerous tax-free manors, but ignoring the political and economic problems which were developing in the provinces. Fortunately, their indulgence in luxury was not limited to mere material splendor, but was directed toward the development of an extremely refined aesthetic culture, so that this age of Lady Murasaki's *Tale of Genji*, has justly been called the golden age of Japanese art and literature: a delicate sensibility and love of nature together with a sure sense of design and color, all of which had previously made themselves felt in Japanese art, were in the Fujiwara Period molded by the hedonistic aestheticism of the courtiers into a decorative art whose sensitive aristocratic beauty is unique in the history of world art (Pl. 6, 40–43, 58–60).

The applied art objects of this period were often sumptuously decorated with naturalistic designs which retained the lyrical beauty and sensuous charm of the natural object without subjecting them to any forced stylization. In no decorative art of any other country is the beauty of nature rendered with such poetic charm as in the pieces reproduced in Plates 43, 59 and 60. This naturalism has retained its hold on Japanese decorative art design down to the present time. Even when the design had to be strongly stylized for functional or technical reasons, the naturalistic tendency often manifested itself in asymmetrical arrangements. Indeed, asymmetry has been a conspicuous design principle in Japanese decorative art since the Fujiwara Period. The floral arabesque engraved on the surface of the sutra box owned by the Enryakuji monastery, dating from the eleventh century (Pl. 40), is an exquisite example of free, asymmetrical arrangement of a stylized arabesque of Chinese origin.

Art of the Fujiwara Period tended toward the exquisite and delicate: it has been seen as almost feminine, possessing neither vigor nor dynamic force. But it was graceful, and reflected an extremely refined sense of proportion (Pl. 41). It aimed at static beauty, avoiding movement; if there was movement, it was very slow and delicate. Full volume was eschewed in favor of a tidy two-dimensionality. These stylistic elements reflect the taste of a court aristocracy which did not lead a very active life, but indulged primarily in aesthetic pastimes. These artistic qualities, however, must have had a much broader and deeper foundation, for the preference for two-dimensionality to full volume, for tidiness to opulence, for serenity to gorgeousness, and most of all for naturalistic decoration to rigidly stylized forms—are the aesthetic vocabulary, not only of this period, but also of many of the periods to follow.

Despite the exquisiteness and delicate beauty of Fujiwara art, any comprehensive view of the art of the period could not fail to reveal that in some branches of applied art, techniques actually retrograded from the high standards of the Nara Period. The brocade became simpler in weave. The technique of gauze-making declined. The less complex processes were probably thought sufficient to achieve the textural effects that were desired in Fujiwara times. People in this period were apparently more concerned with the aesthetic value of colors themselves and their harmony. Court ladies, for instance, took great pains to achieve beautiful color combinations in their formal dresses, which consisted of layers of different colored fabrics. The branch of art which really suffered a serious setback was ceramics. The use of lead color glaze disappeared gradually and was completely discontinued by late Fujiwara times. The production of Sue ware declined. This pottery was replaced by simpler wares with a natural ash glaze which were designed for daily use. They are crude both in form and in the quality of the clay, but the lyricism of the age sometimes facilitated the production of such charming pieces as the urn in Plate 6, which has an engraved design and was excavated at Kawasaki near Yokohama.

While the court aristocrats were absorbed in their hedonistic, aesthetic life, leaving the provincial administration and the management of their manors to the minor officers and the provincial aristocrats, the latter were building up their own military power in the provinces and increasing the number and area of tax-free manors under their own control. Thus there appeared a new class of warrior-aristocrats, with their own estates, independent of the government, and relying for power on their military strength. In order to protect their domains from local enemies, some of them banded together in small local cliques, the leaders of the two strongest being the Taira and the Minamoto. When the court nobility was divided into two factions and engaged in a bitter quarrel, around the middle of the twelfth century, each of these factions sought the support of one of the leading warrior families. After the small civil wars in 1156 and 1160, Kiyomori of the Taira family emerged victorious and the Taira replaced the Fujiwara in their position at court. Having attained the highest position in the Imperial Government, Kiyomori began to enjoy the luxurious court life in Kyoto, and lent his dignity and authority to what may be considered the last glory of Fujiwara art. He officially encouraged the trade with China which had been carried on until that time privately without government sanction. (Incidentally, a Chinese book of the eleventh century mentions a sale of imported Japanese folding fans in China.)

Meanwhile, Yoritomo of the defeated Genji family raised his army in their old family stronghold in eastern Japan and opened hostilities against the Taira in 1180. He overthrew them completely in 1185. Aiming at practical and effective rule over Japan, the victorious Yoritomo did not join the Imperial Government in Kyoto, which by this time did not have any actual power over the provinces. Instead, he established his own military government in Kamakura, three hundred miles east of Kyoto, the easier to control the *samurai* of his clique, whom he appointed either as owners of large estates or as "Protectors" of the various provinces. In this way were laid the foundations of Japanese feudalism, which was to last until modern Japan was born in 1867 A.D.

 ART OF JAPANESE CHIVALRY
(Kamakura Period 1185–1333)

The military class, which had reached a position of dominance, took an active and realistic attitude toward life. This attitude, as well as their vigorous masculine spirit, is reflected in the art of the Kamakura Period. Art became virile: it lost the delicate and static aspect of the art of the previous age, and a realistic, dynamic quality was introduced into painting and sculpture. However, since art always develops out of the conventions of the preceding age, and specifically because the warriors, who previously had had no culture of their own, admired the elaborate culture and elegant life of the court aristocracy (if not their effeminate taste), the decorative art of this period, especially the first part, retained much of the sumptuousness of the art of the previous era. But its delicacy and subtlety disappeared gradually, to be replaced by the virility characteristic of Kamakura taste (Pl. 44–49 and 61–64). This loss of delicacy can be observed not only in design, but also in technique. In the *maki-e* of the Fujiwara Period, subtle color effects and delicate tones had been achieved by using different kinds of metal dust—gold, a pale gold called *aokin*, and silver. But in the Kamakura Period the use of gold dust only, occasionally in combination with mother-of-pearl inlay, was preferred. The appearance of a new technique for making *maki-e* in relief indicates an effort to give the decorative design solidity and strength.

The lacquered "handy" box in Plate 61, with a lyrical representation, in gold *maki-e* and mother-of-pearl inlay, of an autumnal scene with bush-clovers, birds, and deer playing by the riverside, probably dates from the early Kamakura Period. It retains the elegance and lyricism of Fujiwara art, but its composition already suggests the trend toward pictorial naturalism. A more purely pictorial decoration can be seen in the chrysanthemums and fence rendered in mother-of-pearl inlay against a gold background, on the lid of the inkstone box in Plate 62, which probably dates from the first half of the twelfth century. The taste of the high ranking *samurai* for splendor is demonstrated in the brilliant "handy" box with a design of butterflies in gold *maki-e* and mother-of-pearl inlay (Pl. 63), and also in the sumptuous saddle in Plate 64.

It was the warrior-aristocrats of the Fujiwara Period who developed a gorgeous armor with brilliant decorative effects. But the tendency was carried much further by the *samurai* of the Kamakura Period whose sole aspirations to glory lay in a life of warfare. The metal artists worked hard to provide appropriately glorious metal fittings for the armor of the leading military men (Pl. 49). Even in these metal fittings for armor one can see reflected the keen naturalistic sense of the period as well as its taste for splendor, which are also apparent in the reliquary in the Saidaiji monastery (Pl. 47). Another important field of metal art developed for the Japanese warriors was the Japanese sword. Though swords themselves do not fall within the scope of this book, we shall illustrate some later examples of the metal fittings.

Still another important *samurai* contribution to Japanese decorative art was the development of the family crest, the Japanese counterpart of the European coat-of-arms, which played a significant part in the decorative art design of later periods (Pl. 71, 89, 93, and 94). They derive from aristocratic custom of the Fujiwara Period, but it was in this and the following Muromachi Period that most of the family crests we know today were designed for the *samurai*, who needed simple, conspicuous, easily distinguished emblems to put on their banners, arms, draperies, etc. Many of them are masterpieces of design, skillfully abstracting and reducing natural forms to elementary, clear-cut patterns.

From the time Kiyomori began to encourage trade with China at the end of the Fujiwara Period, a closer relationship with the continent gradually developed again, and painting and sculpture of the early Kamakura Period already show a new Chinese influence. But the applied arts were not significantly affected until much later in the period, except in the field of ceramics, which had been least developed before Kamakura times. Chinese brocades were much admired, but the few surviving examples of

Japanese textiles from this period do not show any new Chinese influence; they rather continued to be made in the Fujiwara fashion (Pl. 86).

A great quantity of Chinese celadon and *tenmoku* pottery was imported to Japan during the Kamakura Period, and it was natural that an effort was made, from about the middle of the period, to imitate them at Seto, near Nagoya, where good clay was abundant and a crude ware had been produced since late Fujiwara times. As their technique, however, was not up to such work, the imitation was generally rather unsuccessful. The quality of both the clay and the glaze was poor, the workmanship was crude, and the firing was primitive. The potters did not know much about reducing fire either, and the imitations of Chinese celadon are therefore covered with a yellowish or light greenish-brown glaze (Pl. 7). They have nothing of the elegance and sophisticated beauty of the Chinese originals, but nevertheless they possess a simple, robust charm, which must have appealed to the taste of the Kamakura warriors.

During the second half of this period, the military class gradually developed its own distinctive culture, which, on the one hand, reflected its spartan orientation and, on the other, was greatly influenced by Zen Buddhism. As Zen teaches that reality should be perceived directly by intuition, unencumbered by intellectual or logical constructs, the bonds of the individual ego thereby being broken, the tenets of this sect appealed to the *samurai* who approved of its simplicity and directness, and who found it congenial to the intense military discipline which was so essential to their calling. Zen Buddhism therefore received the patronage of the military leaders of the Kamakura Government, and flourished. A number of Japanese Zen priests visited China to study; several Chinese Zen masters came to Japan to teach. They introduced the Chinese art and literature of the Southern Sung, and later of the Yuan Dynasty, which were greatly influenced by Zen. Although this new cultural influx did not affect Japanese decorative art immediately, it had great consequences in the following period. There was another type of Buddhism which also flourished at this time, supported by simple people of the lower classes. It taught the salvation through the Buddha Amida (Amitabha), which can be achieved by simply chanting his name. As this teaching deliberately avoided elaborate ritualism, its popularity had no effect on the decorative art of the period.

MILITARY CULTURE UNDER ZEN INFLUENCE
(Muromachi Period 1134–1572)

After an attempt, which ultimately failed, by the Emperor Godaigo to regain political control from the Kamakura Government, and a civil war in which all the important warrior-families were involved, the Ashikaga family established their military government in Kyoto, thus replacing the Kamakura Government. Since their headquarters were located at Muromachi in Kyoto, this era is called the Muromachi Period.

Muromachi decorative art was still basically military-oriented, created for the upper-class warriors, especially for the *Shogun* (military governor) of the Ashikaga family and his immediate associates in Kyoto. But the art and culture of the *Shogun's* court, which was under the strong influence

22

of Zen priests, was more "courtly," and decidedly less virile, than that of the preceding age. Decorative art, for example, lost the vigor of the Kamakura Period; but it was also less ostentatious, revealing a more refined, rather sophisticated taste. The technique of lacquer art became more elaborate, not for the purpose of achieving more sumptuous effects, but rather with a view to giving freer reign to the rendering of fine details, and broader scope to the execution of precise workmanship (Pl. 65 and 67). Armor became less showy (Pl. 50), a certain element of elegance and sophistication having been introduced into the complicated patterns of the *odoshi* (threading). For the first time, there appeared a group of metal artists specializing in *tsuba* (sword-guards), which had hitherto been made by the sword-smith. Their work, too, shows a refined and restrained taste (Pl. 56).

The sophisticated Muromachi art which developed in Kyoto eventually spread to the provinces, as there were by this time many powerful feudal lords who could afford it, and who thus helped to develop local art and culture. The bronze lantern in Plate 51, made in one of the eastern provinces for a local war-lord, exhibits a refined taste as well as a highly developed casting technique, neither of which could have been expected from provincial art in earlier periods. In Mino Province there appeared a group of metal artists, experts in the art of chasing, from whom generations of the celebrated Goto family of metal artists were lineally descended (Pl. 55). At Ashiya in Kyushu and at Sano in eastern Japan, a special craft of casting iron kettles was developed (Pl. 52 and 53). Some of the kettles are masterpieces of design, with respect to form, decoration (Pl. 52), and texture. The kettle reproduced in Plate 53 easily rates as a major work of art by virtue of its visual and textural beauty, regardless of whatever functional qualities it may also possess.

A similar appeal, to the touch as well as to the eye, of functional objects viewed as abstract sculptural forms, may be seen in the ceramic wares made at Shigaraki (Shiga Prefecture) and Bizen (Okayama Prefecture) (Pl. 8). Although they were made by simple craftsmen for ordinary daily use, some of these pieces were chosen by tea-ceremony masters, as early as the late fifteenth century, for their rustic beauty, unpretentiousness, simplicity, and the natural quality of their forms. Besides Shigaraki, Bizen, and Seto (which had become by this time great centers of pottery production), there were three other important kilns in Japan during this period: Tamba (Hyogo Prefecture), Echizen (Fukui Prefecture), and Tokoname (Aichi Prefecture). A very early product (from the late Fujiwara Period) of the last named is reproduced in Plate 6. It is interesting to note that, except for Seto, no artificial glaze was used at any of these pottery centers. At Seto, comparatively refined wares covered with artificial glaze were produced; besides the yellowish-brown ash glaze and blackish *tenmoku* glaze, the potters had begun to use a reddish-brown glaze. They also learned to achieve interesting effects through the use of two different glazes on the same piece, one being only partially applied. Many tea-bowls and tea-caddies were produced with these glazes when people started to use Japanese wares for tea-ceremony, from the second half of the fifteenth century.

The fifteenth century is one of the most important in the history of Japanese art, for in that century an entirely new concept of art appreciation made its appearance. Under the guidance of Zen priests, and reflecting the influence of Chinese painting, especially those Zen-oriented works of the Sung and Yuan Dynasties, a preference for spiritual expression to the representation of sensuous beauty came to dominate the artistic consciousness of Japan. Zen teaching elevated the simple love of nature to a profound religious insight. "There is no denying that Zen gave an immense impetus to the Japanese native feeling for nature," says Daisetsu Suzuki, "not only by sharpening it to the highest degree of sensitiveness, but by giving to it a metaphysical and religious background. If in the beginning the Japanese were simply naively attracted to the beautiful which they saw about them … the aesthetic and religious sensitiveness of the Japanese were further given nourishing food as they cultivated themselves in the Zen teaching of Buddhism…. That is to say, the snow-crowned peak of Fuji is now seen as rising from the background of Emptiness" (D. T. Suzuki: *Zen Buddhism and its Influence on Japanese Culture*, 1938, Kyoto, p. 237). The spiritualization of art appreciation, accomplished first in the field of painting, was then expanded into an all-embracing aesthetic attitude which formed the basis of the tea-ceremony (*chanoyu* or *sado* in Japanese). Actually not a ceremony, but an extremely subtle and refined aesthetic pastime to be enjoyed by the host and his guests during the process of preparing and drinking tea, it actually originated as a rather gay form of tea-party, common in the early Muromachi Period, in which *samurai* with some pretension to artistic taste participated. But rules and procedures were gradually formulated, the whole affair being refined in the process.

Chanoyu had become quite formal by the time of ASHIKAGA Yoshimasa (1435–1490), *Shogun* from 1443 to 1473 A.D., but it was the Priest Shuko (1422–1502), a kind of adviser to him in matters pertaining to tea-ceremony after his retirement from the *Shogun's* post, who raised it to a high spiritual-aesthetic plain, imbuing it with his Zen spirit. He established rules and formulas for room decoration, the arrangement and the types of utensils to be used, and for the procedures to be followed, even down to the movements of the host in serving tea, all of which were to be so designed as to enable the participants to immerse themselves deeply into the profound aesthetic experience of the "ceremony." *Chanoyu* was further developed by his successors, particularly TAKE no Joo (1503–1555), in the late Muromachi Period. The spiritual ideals toward which these tea-masters aimed were: harmony, respect (for things and persons), cleanliness (physical and spiritual) and tranquility (or quietude). The aesthetic ideal and artistic quality which they sought were *wabi* and *sabi*, respectively, concepts which are deeply rooted in Zen.

Wabi literally means insufficiency, the "inability to fulfill every desire one may cherish" (Daisetsu Suzuki); it is the aesthetic appreciation of insufficiency without the feeling of inadequacy. It also sometimes refers to the aesthetic quality which evokes such a reaction. *Sabi* literally indicates quietude, a sense of loneliness, and signifies the beauty inherent in such a state. TAKE no Joo said that "the *wabi* spirit of *chanoyu* is the spirit of the following old *waka* (thirty-one syllable poem) by FUJIWARA Sadaie:

> When going out, and looking:
> Cherry blossoms nor maple leaves—
> None at all:
> Lonely hut—
> Autumn evening."

Wabi, then, is the aesthetic experience whereby the sense of transience or emptiness (*sabi*) becomes an ecstacy.

Alan W. Watts writes in his *The Way of Zen:* "Transitoriness is depressing only to the mind which insists upon trying to grasp. But to the mind which lets go and moves with the flow of change, which becomes, in Zen Buddhist imagery, like a ball in a mountain stream, the sense of transience or emptiness becomes a kind of ecstasy." (Mentor Book ed., p. 52.) Thus, if one is aware of the reality in the very transitoriness of life, he can derive aesthetic satisfaction from the actual aspect of nature and life stripped of their illusory and transient beauty, which attitude, however, is not necessarily accompanied by the abhorrence of sensuous beauty, as long as it is truly natural. For the Japanese, it was not difficult to attain to such a philosophical aesthetic position under the influence of Zen, since the older Buddhist sects had been cultivating the Japanese mind in that direction for a long time.

But we must not assume that all the tea-ceremony masters understood *wabi* and *sabi* in their truest, most profound sense. Once these aesthetic ideas were formulated under Zen influence, it was relatively easy, even for those uninitiated in Zen, to appreciate the more superficial aspects of the austere beauty of arts based on these aesthetic modes. Tea-ceremony became a vogue among the war-lords and rich merchants in the following Momoyama Period, and exercised a tremendous influence on its ceramic art.

 ## AGE OF VIGOR AND MAGNIFICENCE
(Momoyama Period 1573–1614)

Politically, the fourteenth and fifteenth centuries were a period of the growth of powerful feudal lords (*daimyo*). As their power grew it became difficult for the Muromachi Government to control them, and political chaos was already dominant by the latter half of the fifteenth century. During the first seventy years of the sixteenth century, full-scale civil wars were fought among virtually independent feudal lords; the *Shogun*, whose power was practically nil, was more or less ignored. On the other hand, trade and industry expanded greatly in these two centuries, and developed further during the civil wars, which encouraged the growth of big merchants who could deal with the feudal lords on a large scale.

At the close of the civil wars, which resulted in the downfall of the Ashikaga family and its military government, ODA Nobunaga emerged as victorious war-lord, but was soon thereafter assassinated by one of his generals. He was succeeded by another general, Hideyoshi, who finally managed to unify Japan. Both Nobunaga and Hideyoshi were men of great talent and ambition, who liked to have everything done on a grand scale, and the dominant, expansive character of both these men undoubtedly had considerable influence on the art of this period, as they lavishly spent money for the decoration of huge castles and the embellishment of their surroundings.

The period of civil wars was one of great activity. If he had talent and ambition, a foot-soldier could become a general, even the lord of a large territory. This was what actually happened to Hideyoshi. And if a merchant were smart enough, he could carry on an extremely profitable business with the feudal lords. If he were adventurous, he could make considerable profits from over-seas trade, which was very lively at the time. At Hakata in Kyushu and in the town of Sakai, a port close to Osaka, there were many rich merchants who made a good deal of money out of foreign trade, which by the end of the Muromachi Period extended as far as Southeast Asia. In short, the whole of Japan was stirred to action during the civil wars; an active, virile, adventurous spirit was nurtured, and many daring, large-minded figures appeared. Nobunaga and Hideyoshi were the ideals of the age. After Hideyoshi restored peace to Japan, this active, virile spirit burst out in every field of activity in the Momoyama Period. Foreign trade continued to thrive, and a great quantity of foreign articles was imported. Huge castles and gorgeous palaces (Pl. 54) with vast rooms and halls were built. Their walls and sliding-doors were sumptuously decorated. Life became gay, bright, and luxurious. People of both the warrior and merchant classes wore brilliant, showy costumes, and wealthy women's attire, which had by this time developed into the type called *kosode* (see the explanatory note to Pl. 92), the basic form out of which today's *kimono* was derived, was lavishly decorated with dyed and embroidered designs, and often embellished with pasted gold and silver foil (Pl. 92 and 93). Even the men of the period liked to wear gay, colorful costumes with large, bold designs, a tendency which had already developed during the civil wars at the close of the Muromachi Period (Pl. 88 and 89). And the large patterns on the *kosode* were dyed with a special tie-and-dye technique that had been used since the second half of that period (Pl. 90, 92, 94 and 95). This luxurious life and taste for brilliance led to the production of such rich textile fabrics, employing advanced weaving techniques newly learned from China, as gold brocade, satin, satin damask, and *crepe de Chine*.

The *maki-e* of the period is decorative and sumptuous, although no particularly elaborate technique was utilized. The designs are naturalistic, but not so pictorial as those of middle Kamakura and Muromachi Period *maki-e*. Flowering branches and grass sprays in gold *maki-e* are decoratively arranged on black lacquered surfaces, yielding opulent (but never merely flashy), eye-pleasing effects (Pl. 69 and 70). Although many of the design motifs were taken from late Fujiwara decorative art, there is no such lyricism as was to be found in Fujiwara *maki-e*, as Momoyama designs generally tend to be very bold. The so-called "Meigetsu bowls" (Pl. 72), with mother-of-pearl inlay, are simple in both workmanship and taste (they were donated to a Zen monastery), but are nonetheless vigorous in design and gorgeous in effect. Some *maki-e* designs make use of European motifs—a result of foreign trade and the missionary work of the Jesuits.

Fujiwara lyricism would have been of little interest to the lively, vigorous people of this age. They appreciated gaiety and splendor, but also, contradictory though it may seem, the austerity of *wabi* and *sabi*. Hideyoshi, who built gorgeous palaces and lived in vast, sumptuously decorated rooms, was at the same time an ardent devotee of the *wabi* tea-ceremony: he was a diligent pupil of SEN no Rikyu (1522–1591), the great tea-ceremony master and aesthete of *wabi*, for more than ten years.* These apparently conflicting orientations were shared by many minor war-lords and rich merchants. Though they used such lacquer wares as those mentioned above, and wore gay *kosode* in their daily life, they prized simple, rustic ceramic wares once they entered the small, unpretentious tea-ceremony room, built in the fashion of a poor farmer's hut, where they sought relief from the hustle and bustle

---

* Hideyoshi became displeased with the "insolent" behavior of Rikyu in early 1591 and subsequently ordered him to kill himself.

of the everyday world. Thus, the *wabi* tea-ceremony thrived in the otherwise flamboyant Momoyama Period. The devotees of *chanoyu*, with their *wabi* taste, ultimately brought about the first golden age of Japanese ceramic art in this period (Pl. 9 and 16). It was Rikyu who directed the potter Chojiro of the Raku kiln in Kyoto to produce magnificent tea-bowls with rustic yet mellow texture, and forms which are both graceful and powerful in their sense of volume (Pl. 16–18). The size, shape, thickness and the quality of clay in these vessels are perfectly combined to maintain the warmth of the tea without allowing the bowl to become too hot to hold between the palms while drinking. In short, they are functional. But, at the same time, they have an aesthetic appeal, not only to the eye, but also to the touch, as they are handled and held in the course of the tea-ceremony. Chojiro was succeeded by several gifted potters and his tradition has continued to the present in the Raku kiln.

Another great tea-ceremony master, FURUTA Oribe (1544–1615), who was incidentally one of Hideyoshi's generals, guided the potters of Mino Province (a part of today's Gifu Prefecture) with his orders and advice. They produced Ki-Seto (Pl. 9), Shino (Pl. 10–12) and Oribe (Pl. 13 and 14) wares in this period and in the earliest part of the next period. The latter two types, Shino and Oribe, especially reflect the vigorous spirit of the time, and the austere taste of a tea-ceremony master who also had an extremely fine sensibility for beautiful things. The same master is said to have given his counsel to the potters of the Iga kiln, in present-day Mie Prefecture, which produced strong, rustic wares, attractively deformed, and marked with accidental streaks of the ash glaze (Pl. 15). Wares for *chanoyu* with a *sabi* aesthetic were also produced—at Seto, Bizen, and Shigaraki.

When Hideyoshi undertook his unsuccessful invasion of Korea, his generals brought back Korean potters with them to their own domains. Those who settled down in Hizen Province (Saga Prefecture) began, at the close of this period, to produce lovely Korean-type pottery. As their oldest principle kiln was located south of Karatsu, their wares are called Karatsu (Pl. 19 and 20). At other places in Kyushu, too, where Korean potters settled ceramic production started; but these kilns came to eminence only in the early part of the following Edo Period, except for the one started by the potter Kin Kai in Satsuma Province (Kagoshima Prefecture), which produced attractive tea-ceremony wares for the local feudal lord, SHIMAZU Yoshihiro (Pl. 21).

 ## Art for Samurai and Merchants
(Edo Period 1615–1867)

Hideyoshi did not set up his own military government, but controlled the other feudal lords by holding a kind of civil dictator's position on Imperial appointment. The power structure he had constructed, however, was toppled after his death by TOKUGAWA Ieyasu, a powerful feudal lord from eastern Japan. Ieyasu established his own military government (Bakufu) in Edo (present-day Tokyo), where he laid the firm foundations of a well-organized feudalistic system which could be controlled for generations by his descendants. The Tokugawa Bakufu maintained domestic peace for two and a half centuries; "unfortunately, they secured peace and stability by a series of rigid controls over society, by ruthless suppression of many of the most creative tendencies in the Japan of that day, and by a return to many of the outmoded forms of feudalism" (Edwin O. Reischauer: *Japan, Past and Present*, Tuttle ed., p. 80).

Japan was secluded again from the outer world. Christianity was prohibited. No trade, or even communication was permitted with foreign countries, except for some contact with Holland and China, trade with these two countries being allowed only at the port of Nagasaki, under strict government control. While Confucianism was adopted as an official philosophy and Chinese classic literature was highly esteemed, the study of Western culture was discouraged. A rigid hierarchy sharply divided the four social classes, with the warrior (*samurai*) at the top, followed in order by the farmer, the craftsman, and the merchant. There was not much incentive for individual creative activity, and the adventurous, daring spirit of the Momoyama Period gradually disappeared.

However, during the very early part (the first fifty years) of this period, while the rigid feudalistic system was still in the process of formation, the active and virile tone was not yet dead: the vigor and splendor of Momoyama art survived, though in a somewhat restrained form, through the first half of the seventeenth century. Patronized by the rising Tokugawa family, by the great feudal lords, and by the wealthy heads of merchant houses, the decorative arts of this brief period were sumptuous —perhaps not so grandiose as those of the previous period, but more sophisticated in both style and workmanship (Pl. 18, 21, 73, 74, 76, 93, 94 and 96). The so-called "Hatsune Set" of lacquered furniture (Pl. 73) is an example of decorative art work done for the reigning Tokugawa family by Nagashige (1599–1651) of the Koami family, which had maintained a family tradition of elaborate *maki-e* technique since the Muromachi Period. The "Hidehira Bowls," on the other hand, are a provincial work, but their design is nevertheless vigorous and gorgeous (Pl. 74).

There was in the same early Edo Period another, entirely different, style of decorative art which suggests a more refined, "classic" taste, the revival of a Fujiwara Period aesthetic, though modified by the vigorous, masculine spirit of early Edo times. This style was especially favored by the court aristocrats and rich merchants in Kyoto. The leader of the artistic trend was Koetsu (1558–1637), a great calligrapher and distinguished aesthete of many talents. At a place called Takagamine, near Kyoto, given to him by Ieyasu, he established a village of artists of different crafts, to whom he gave advice and supplied his own brilliant designs (Pl. 76). He also made pottery of unusual beauty himself, and one of his tea bowls is illustrated in Plate 18. The applied art objects he designed, and/or made, are the aesthetic peers of the period's greatest masterpieces of painting and sculpture. For this great aesthete, as for his close associate Sotatsu, the creator of a new decorative style in painting, anything to be looked at was subject to the highest standards of formal, textural, and representational beauty. His stylized design of various motifs from nature (Pl. 76) is not a product of forced stylization for a decorative purpose; it consists rather of directly perceived aesthetic factors, reduced to their essentials, and arranged so as to accommodate the form of the object most satisfyingly. Koetsu's decorative style, as well as his artistic ideals, were inherited by OGATA Korin (1658–1716) in the middle Tokugawa Period.

The feudal system of the Tokugawa Bakufu depended heavily upon the activities of merchants, notwithstanding the hierarchy in which the latter were placed at the very bottom. The actual economic

28

power of the merchant class increased greatly during the seventeenth century, and they became a significant, influential social force, not only economically but also culturally. And in addition to the feudal lords and the great merchants, the middle-class *samurai* (retainers of the feudal lords) and the middle-class merchants also became patrons of art. The social basis of the decorative arts was thus greatly expanded.

The Tokugawa Government had its own large workshop of craftsmen to produce the applied art objects for the use of the Tokugawa family and the government. And other feudal lords followed this pattern: most notable was MAEDA Tsunanori (1643–1722), the lord of Kaga Province and one of the wealthiest figures of his time. He organized a large factory (an establishment similar to the Gobelin Factory in France) for producing all kinds of decorative art objects; he invited skilled craftsmen from other provinces, and exerted great efforts to advance the applied arts industry in his domain. Thus encouraged by the feudal lords, the decorative arts thrived during the middle and late Edo Period— at least in terms of quantity and technique, if not artistically. The decorative art objects of this age, produced in great quantities by many craftsmen, tended toward conventionality, but there were nevertheless many master craftsmen with ingenuity and an excellent sense of design.

As has already been mentioned, Koetsu's style was continued and further developed by OGATA Korin, one of Japan's greatest painters, who also made designs for lacquer works (Pl. 77) and other applied art objects, including *kimono*. His art greatly influenced all the decorative arts of his own as well as later periods. Many pieces of lacquer ware of the eighteenth and nineteenth centuries were decorated in the "Korin style." However, as the craftsmen of the Edo Period were ingenious designers, and as their customers came from various social backgrounds and possessed a broad range of artistic taste, the lacquer art of this period is versatile in both style and technique (Pl. 75, 78–81). Some *maki-e* decorations were quite naturalistic, such as those in Plate 81, and there were more naturalistic designs even than these: executed in all possible techniques of *maki-e*, with a variety of metal dusts, they almost give the impression of paintings. Beside the *maki-e*, colored lacquer and color pigment mixed with oil were used, primarily in the case of cheaper wares, for decoration on lacquered grounds (Pl. 75 and 80). The furniture reproduced in Plate 78, an ingeniously combined chest of drawers and screen, is a good example of the beautiful furniture design of the period.

A special genre of lacquer art which flourished at this time was the *inro*, a nest of small boxes carried by men, suspended from the belt, and containing a seal or medicine (Pl. 81). From the late seventeenth century, *samurai* vied with one another in the beauty, elaborate workmanship, and ingenuity of design of their *inro*. Feudal lords and high-ranking *samurai* spent tremendous sums of money on this miniature art, a case roughly analogous to that of snuff-boxes in eighteenth century Europe. The *inro* was hung from the belt by a cord, and to prevent this cord from slipping out of the belt, a small object, called *netsuke*, was tied at the other end of the cord. These *netsuke* were also used by merchants for carrying tobacco pouches, writing implements, etc. They became an important minor art, but as most of the *netsuke* come under the category of miniature sculpture, we do not treat the form in this book.

Korin's brother, Kenzan (1663–1743), brought Korin's decorative style into pottery (Pl. 28 and 29). Kenzan was preceded in Kyoto by another great ceramic artist, NONOMURA Ninsei (active in the second half of the seventeenth century), who excelled in the use of the pottery wheel, by which he produced magnificent shapes; he also mastered the effective use of various kinds of glaze, and decorated his wares with delightful designs in colored enamel (Pl. 27). Over-glaze enamel color was used by him for the first time in Kyoto, which became one of the most important Japanese ceramic art centers later, in the eighteenth century. The earliest use in Japan of this coloring technique was in the 1640's at Arita in Kyushu, where a Korean potter had succeeded in producing Japan's first true porcelain in the early Edo Period. Many Japanese potters followed his example and began to produce procelain. At first their wares were decorated only in under-glaze blue (Pl. 22), but during the 1640's, SAKAIDA Kakiemon succeeded in rendering over-glaze color enamel designs. He and his successors developed a unique type of color decoration, known the world over as the Kakiemon style (Pl. 23). Kakiemon wares were exported by Dutch traders and highly prized in Europe in the late seventeenth and all through the eighteenth century. His color enamel was soon imitated by other potters in and around Arita, where a great porcelain industry developed. These Arita wares were shipped from the port of Imari, and are thus commonly referred to as Imari wares.

The secrets of porcelain and color enamel decoration were then stolen by the potters of the Kutani kiln in Ishikawa Prefecture, who managed to produce, in the second half of the seventeenth century, a porcelain possessing a powerful, masculine beauty, with daring designs in a color-scheme which is quite different from that of the wares made in Kyushu (Pl. 25). The production of porcelain at Kutani was discontinued around 1700, but was revived in the early nineteenth century. The district around Kutani has since become one of the three main centers of the Japanese porcelain industry, in addition to Arita and Seto, the latter having also started to produce porcelain in the early nineteenth century. Among other porcelain kilns which developed at different places in the middle and late Edo Period, the Nabeshima kiln at Okochi, near Arita, was artistically the most important. The kiln was run by the house of Nabeshima, the local feudal lords, and produced porcelain wares of the finest quality exclusively for the family's use and for gifts (Pl. 24). Its extremely refined clay, precise workmanship and cold, sophisticated beauty are unique in Japanese porcelain.

In this period, the *samurai* prided themselves on the beauty of their sword mountings, and the art of making *tsuba* (sword-guards) (Pl. 56), as well as other sword fittings, such as *kozuka*, *kogai*, and *menuki* (refer to the explanation of Pl. 55) developed apace. Many local schools of metal artists grew up as each feudal lord encouraged this industry as a *samurai* art.

As the people began to enjoy a settled, peaceful life, and as the standard of living rose, especially among the merchants, the ladies' *kosode* became more decorative, often quite flamboyant, though they were rarely so grandiose in conception as those of the Momoyama Period; men's dress, on the other hand, became more somber and austere. In addition to, or rather in place of, the *tsujigahana*, there developed in the early Edo Period another type of tie-and-dye technique called *hitta*, which was capable of achieving rich, gay effects, both in color and texture (Pl. 94 and 95). A little later, around the middle of the seventeenth century, another new technique of dyeing designs was developed, which greatly affected later feminine attire, because it permitted the dyeing of *kimono* with free, multi-colored pictorial designs. The new technique used rice-paste as a resist to the dye. The use of wax as a resist had been known in the Nara Period, but had been discontinued during the next period. Perhaps it was the rediscovery of *batik* that led Japanese craftsmen to try rice-paste, instead of wax, as a dye resist. At any rate the technique was occasionally used in Japan for stencil dyeing as early as the sixteenth century. Then, toward the middle of the seventeenth century, some craftsmen, elaborating the technique, began to apply the rice-paste by hand with a kind of paper-tube and a stick, so that complicated, detailed designs could be covered by the paste. At first the cloth was dyed in only one color—blue (Pl. 101); but by the last quarter of the seventeenth century the method had been applied to the dyeing of multi-colored designs. Except for the ground color, the different colored dyes came to be applied by brush. This polychrome dyeing method utilizing rice-paste is called *yuzen-zome* (Pl. 103 and 104).

In the late seventeenth century, ladies' costumes became even more spectacular, and the *obi* (sash) became wider and more luxurious; accordingly, brocade and tapestry weaving flourished in Kyoto. And during the eighteenth century, many types of elaborate silk weaving developed in other localities also.

Stencil-dyeing, using rice-paste as a dye resist, was employed in its early stages to furnish cloth to suit the *samurai's* simple, masculine taste. A fine, detailed geometric design was dyed in a single color (Pl. 105), this type of stencil dyeing being called *komon*, or "small pattern." Another type of stencil dyeing with larger designs, called *chugata*, was developed to dye simple cotton *kimono* for both men and women (Pl. 106).

The cultivation of cotton had already started in Japan by the late Muromachi Period, but it was only in the early Edo Period that production became extensive enough to permit consumption by the common people, who until that time had had to depend on hemp cloth for their clothing. By the late eighteenth century the art of cotton weaving had advanced considerably. Since the wearing of silk was sometimes forbidden to the merchants (though such regulations, being practically unenforceable, soon became obsolete), wealthy members of that class would indulge themselves by elaborating the design and workmanship of cotton *kimono*, or by contriving some hidden luxury; some people, for example, prided themselves on their ostensibly simple cotton *kimono*, which were, however, lined with expensive silk woven in complex patterns. *Chugata* stencil dyeing of cotton material was developed and elaborated; its lively, often humorous designs, while in the national tradition of clear, tidy patterns, also reflect the animation and sturdiness of the common people, who perhaps had to live under the yoke of the *samurai*, but nevertheless possessed a strength and self-confidence born of the ability to earn their own living (Pl. 107).

The *samurai's* economy depended on the income he derived from the rice produced by the farmers in his domain. In order to exchange this rice for money, the feudal lords had to sell their rice through the merchants, who became wealthier as time went on, and finally acquired a position of economic control, while both the Tokugawa Government and the feudal lords fell into financial difficulties. To restore economic balance, they had recourse only to frugality, or to exploitation of the farmers. The only other possibility was to borrow money from the wealthy merchants. By the middle of the nineteenth century, as these financial problems and unrest among the farmers had weakened the Tokugawa Government tremendously, although the administrative organization still appeared to function smoothly enough, there arose a movement to restore actual authority to the Emperor. And just at that time, foreign pressure from the West began to mount. Thus, internal and external stresses finally compelled the Tokugawa family to dissolve its military government and, in 1867, to "return" authority to the Emperor, around whom a new government was organized. Japanese feudalism was brought to an end.

 OLD JAPAN AND NEW JAPAN
(Modern Age 1868–   )

The Emperor's Court was moved to Edo, which was renamed Tokyo, and the central government established there. To cope with Japan's new vulnerability *vis-a-vis* the outside world, the new government was firmly resolved on a policy of "modernizing" Japan by the introduction of Western civilization. This they did at an amazingly rapid pace: Japan was "modernized" and her industrial revolution accomplished in the relatively brief period of the reign of Emperor Meiji (1867–1911), by the rapid-fire adoption of one phase of Western civilization after another—political and economic systems, technology and the sciences, and even literature and the arts—rarely with any attempt to integrate the new elements with the traditional culture, which continued to exist side by side with the newly imported, mechanically grafted Western culture.

Japan was then faced with the difficult cultural problem of how to integrate these two different elements and create a new modern culture based on her own national traditions and cultural orientations. Almost a century after the Meiji Restoration she is still struggling with this problem.

The common confusion between the concepts of modernization and Westernization compounded the difficulty. While the "progressives" were busily absorbing the superficial aspects of Western culture and importing all its most current fads, the traditionally-minded tended to be reactionary, holding to the conventions of feudal Japan without trying to revitalize them with any new spirit. There has always been, however, a minority movement that has sought to create a new culture, which would rest firmly on national traditions and yet take full cognizance of contemporary living conditions and be thoroughly modern in outlook; fortunately, this movement has shown signs in recent years of making itself felt in a variety of different fields.

Japan's post-feudal cultural dilemma is naturally reflected in her modern decorative arts. Economic, if not artistic, success has followed in the wake of the industrialization of the applied arts; this was accomplished by the wholesale adoption of Western techniques, manufacturing methods, and even designs. The textile industry, for instance—both weaving and dyeing (printing)—underwent an enormous expansion; but this industrial success was achieved at the expense of the abandonment of Japanese decorative art traditions altogether. In 1959, Japan produced $123,184,000 worth of porcelain and other pottery wares, about 70 percent of which was exported. The ceramic industry has fared a little better artistically than the textile industry, but not much. A majority of its porcelain products have designs which are either purely Western or easy, and usually unimaginative, compromises between Western and traditional motifs. The possibilities of "Good Design" in industrial arts based on Japanese tradition are now being seriously studied by designers, but, unfortunately, not so much by manufacturers. On the other hand, the commercial lacquer ware industry, which has organized the handicraft on a mass-production basis by the division of labor, has been rather faithful to traditional design: so faithful, in fact, that the art has degenerated into a dreary conventionality.

Efforts have been made by a number of individual modern artists in the traditional handicrafts to develop their arts in terms of modern concepts. But it must be admitted that most of their works are artistically uninteresting, despite their good intentions and elaborate techniques, being either unimaginatively conventional or superficially Western. Nevertheless, there have been, and are, a considerable number of artists who are creating handsome applied art objects, which, in addition to being functional, are true to Japan's traditions, and can be appreciated as objects of aesthetic enjoyment. However, as these modern decorative art works really deserve an extensive treatment of their own, it has been thought best not to touch on them in this volume.

It is difficult to extrapolate from the history of Japanese decorative art those characteristics which are peculiarly and essentially Japanese. For one thing, Japanese art, like all other arts, has passed through a number of different phases of historical development, and it is all too easy to accept, as basically Japanese, characteristics which are in fact peculiar, or at least of special relevance, to a particular period; this is especially likely in the case of Japan's last age of feudalism, the Edo Period, with which we are most familiar. For instance, the *shibui* (restrained, refined) aesthetic ideal reflected the sophisticated, refined taste of wealthy merchants, who financially could afford any luxury, but had to restrain themselves because of the various restrictions and regulations imposed on them by the Tokugawa Government. Is this ideal to be viewed as the expression of a fundamental Japanese aesthetic principle, or as one bi-product of the Edo Period feudal system? Or is it perhaps both?

In this introduction, an attempt has been made to indicate the distinctive character of each period, and to suggest the aesthetic orientation which underlies and defines each period's decorative arts. Nevertheless, certain artistic altitudes seem to run through all these stages of Japanese art history. With Laurence Binyon, we can observe a "national instinct for fastidious and clear order." A profound love of nature is also apparent in all periods; different from the Western love of nature, it is based on the particularly Far Eastern view of man as an integral part of the universe. This and the extraordinary Japanese sensitivity to the beauty of nature have been demonstrated time and again in the preceding pages by the strong preference on the part of Japanese decorative artists for non-stylized naturalistic designs. The same aesthetic reliance on nature can be seen in the extremely subtle and skillful use of materials so as to reveal their beauty and natural qualities to the best advantage.

To the extent that these artistic considerations no longer govern the production and choice of functional objects in Japan today, one can only regret their passing. But we may still hope that the works represented in this volume can serve as inspiration to those of us, in Japan as well as the rest of the world, who in their everyday lives would still prefer to be using beautiful things.

CHISABUROH F. YAMADA

33

陶芸

Ceramics

1

JOMON pottery is the oldest type of earthenware found in Japan. Carbon tests prove that the Jomon vessels excavated in Yokosuka, Kanagawa Prefecture, date back to 7,000 B.C. It could, thus, be claimed that they are the oldest known pottery in the world.

This type of piece is referred to as the *kaengata* (flame-type) from its appearance, and was made in the middle Jomon Period. The earthenware of this period is characterized by the thickness of the vessels and decorative patterns of clay attached to the surface Vessels with such exaggerated ornamentation are found mainly in central and eastern Japan.

The skill with which the rather grainy clay is handled is particularly evident in the relief-like design on the lower half of the vessel, in the handles resembling bird heads affixed symmetrically near its mouth, and in the band of waves decorating its brim. Despite the ornamental excellence of the piece, it is doubtful whether it ever actually functioned as a container.

This piece was excavated in Umadaka, Sekigahara-machi, Nagaoka City, Niigata Prefecture.

縄文

火焰形土器

Kaengata-doki (Flame-type Earthenware)
Height: 29.5 cm.
Middle-Jomon Period
Owned by: Nagaoka Municipal Science Museum,
Niigata Prefecture

2

THE YAYOI Period (roughly 300 B.C. to 300 A.D.) culture was marked by significant advances over the Jomon culture. Rice growing, for instance, was learned from the Asian mainland. Pieces of the earthenware of this period were excavated in 1884 in Yayoi-cho, Tokyo; hence the name.

This Yayoi jar is encircled by bands of delicate feather-shaped designs, and round clay plates are attached at the edge of the mouth. Red coloring has been achieved by painting the jar with a mixture of soft mud and iron powder, which oxidizes and turns red when fired. The edges of the red bands are fringed with knotted *jomon* rope patterns, which accent the design.

Such patterns are widespread in earthenware found in the southern Kanto area. Jars like the one illustrated here were used to store grain and other foodstuff. They are believed to have been made by women, without the use of hand wheels, and to have been fired in the open.

弥生

丹塗壺

Ninuri Tsubo (*Red Colored Jar*)
Height: 39.5 cm.
Late Yayoi Period
Private Collection

38

3

SUE POTTERY was produced in Japan extensively and uninterruptedly from the fifth to the thirteenth century. The usual Sue pot is of a dark shade, gray or blackish-gray, and sounds metallic when tapped. Sue pottery was the first to be molded on hand-wheels, and would also seem to have been the first to be produced by specialized potters. More than 2,000 pieces have been discovered so far. This jar, whose bulging body and elevated base are typical of Nara and Heian Period Sue pottery, is thought to have been influenced by the round jars of the T'ang Dynasty in China. The ashes that settled on the shoulders of the vessel in the firing process formed a natural thick olive-colored glaze which was allowed to drip down the sides.

40

須恵器

壺

Sue Ware Jar
Height: 26.3 cm.
Body Diameter: 30.4 cm.
Nara Period
Owned by: Matsunaga Memorial Hall, Odawara,
Kanagawa Prefecture

4

NARA SANSAI (three-color) pottery was the earliest to be coated with artificial glaze. The color and texture of the glaze of this jar, fired at low-temperature, are quite similar to those of T'ang three-color ware. But the shape, material, and the technique of manufacture are distinctive enough to establish its Japanese origin conclusively. It was excavated from the foot of Mt. Daishokusan, near Osaka, in 1907. Low-fired pottery of the Nara and Heian Periods has been excavated throughout Japan during the past 30 years, but this is the most excellent of the Nara Sansai pieces.

Having been buried for such a long time, the glazed surface of the body is quite corroded, but the white, reddish-brown, and green low-temperature glazes of the cover are in good condition. The inside of the vessel is coated with a light-greenish tinted low-temperature white glaze. The back of the base is unglazed.

Archaeologists claim that it was a funeral urn, but whether that was its original purpose is not clear.

奈良三彩

共蓋壺

Nara Sansai Jar with Matching Cover
Height: 15.7 cm.
Body Diameter: 21 cm.
Nara Period
Important Cultural Property
Owned by: Tokyo National Museum

43

5

THERE ARE 57 ceramic wares of low-temperature glaze, commonly referred to as the Shosoin Sansai (Shosoin three-color ware), in the Nanso, or southern storehouse, of the Shosoin repository. However, there are only five items actually glazed in three colors. Numerically, the largest group (35) consists of green and white two-color, or Nisai, pieces.

This bowl is typical of Nisai ware in form as well as in glaze tone, which is amazingly fresh even after 1,200 years. There is a black ink inscription under the base with a year corresponding to 755 A.D. and the name of Todaiji monastery.

There used to be a theory that the Shosoin Sansai were made in China, but it has since been established that they were actually Japanese products.

The material of the body is a clay identical to that of the grayish-white roof tiles of the Nara Period. This clay was covered with a low-temperature green glaze derived from copper, and in the spots untouched by the green there is a white glaze.

正倉院二彩 平鉢

Shosoin Nisai Flat Bowl
Height: 7.7 cm.
Diameter: 20.7 cm.
Nara Period
Preserved in: Shosoin Repository, Nara

44

6

DURING the Kamakura and Muromachi Periods, there were kilns in Seto, Tokoname, Shigaraki, Tanba, Echizen, and Bizen. These are often referred to as the "six old kiln sites" of Japan. Of these, Tokoname was probably the most extensive. Remains of approximately 1,000 kilns have been discovered within the 2.5 mile by 12.5 mile Chita Peninsula strip centered around Tokoname. From the Heian Period, farmers of this region have made jars for daily use which were exported to other parts of Japan.

This urn, with a pattern of autumn plants scored on its body, was unearthed in Kawasaki City, Kanagawa Prefecture, in 1942. It contained ashes at the time of discovery.

The base material is a coarse grayish clay, which was covered with the natural glaze that dripped down the sides in several lines. The step at the lower portion of the neck serves to distinguish the piece as a Heian product. On the trunk of the jar are three clusters of Japanese pampas grass; on the shoulders are incised cucumber, willow, pampas grass, straight line, and leaf patterns; on the neck are more straight lines and pampas grass designs, as well as a dragonfly. On the inside of the mouth a Japanese character is incised.

46

古常滑 秋草文壺

Old Tokoname Ware Jar with Autumn Plant Design
Height: 40 cm.
Body Diameter: 29 cm.
Fujiwara Period
National Treasure
Owned by: Keio University, Tokyo

47

7

ARTIFICIAL high-temperature glaze was applied to pottery from the Heian Period on. The glaze was first obtained by covering the surface with ashes. A more reliable form of high-temperature glaze was attained in Seto in the Kamakura Period by the addition of feldspar. There are remains of more than 200 kilns in the Seto area dating from the Heian to the Muromachi Periods.

The shape of this vessel is reminiscent of the light green celadon porcelain vases produced at the *Ching Teh Cheng* kilns of China in the Southern Sung Period. The design, technique and glaze, however, are typical of Seto district kilns, this jar being a representative product of the Hyakume kiln in Akazu, which fired exceptionally high quality pottery during the Kamakura Period.

The base material is a grayish-white, hard, semi-porcelaneous clay, to which was applied a comparatively thick, light yellowish-brown glaze. There is a tongue of dark amber-colored iron glaze on the side, which appears to have been caused accidently during firing. Small irruptions cover the entire surface, on which peony and arabesque molds have been impressed. The bottom is flat and unglazed.

48

古瀬戸

牡丹唐草文瓶

Old Seto Ware Jar with Peony and Arabesque Designs
Height: 24.3 cm.
Body Diameter: 16.6 cm.
Late Kamakura Period
Private Collection

8

BIZEN pottery has a history of more than a thousand years. It is a hard, dark, dull-textured ware, made of a clay that contains a large amount of iron; the surface is often covered with a natural ash glaze by the high-temperature firing itself, without the addition of any artificial coating.

Bizen wares—vases, water containers, tea bowls, tea pots, incense containers, etc.—with *hidasuki* (crossed flame) patterns, made during the Momoyama Period, are especially highly valued.

This water container with *hidasuki* patterns on its body is representative of the Momoyama ware. The patterns were made by tying straws to the body, so that only these portions bear red scorched marks, which stand out against the grayish-white surface.

The intentionally somewhat warped shape is also typical of Momoyama style. The bottom is flat.

古備前

火襷水指

Old Bizen Hidasuki Water Container
Height: 13.5 cm.
Mouth Diameter: 13 cm.
Body Diameter: 16 cm.
Important Cultural Property
Momoyama Period
Private Collection

9

KI-SETO or "yellow" Seto ware was made in Gifu Prefecture during the Momoyama Period. There are two general types: the *guinomi-de* with a yellow transparent glaze, and the *aburage-de* with a dull glaze and rough texture. The dish illustrated here is of the latter type. The remains of more than ten Ki-Seto kiln sites of this period have been found in Kani and Dogi Counties in Gifu Prefecture, but the most outstanding pieces were produced by the Kamashita kilns at Okaya.

This dish was used for serving cakes in the tea-ceremony. Ki-Seto fragments of the same quality, found in the remains of the Kamashita kilns, bear dates corresponding to 1593, and this piece was probably made about the same time.

The base material is a coarse egg-shell colored clay, which was coated with a dull, light brownish-yellow glaze. Iris designs are incised with simple lines and a bluish-green glaze is applied to the leaves.

黄瀬戸　あやめ文鉢

Ki-Seto Cake Dish with Iris Design
Height: 8.3 cm.
Diameter: 25.3 cm.
Momoyama Period
Private Collection

53

10

SHINO is a white-glazed pottery which was first made in Japan during the Momoyama Period. There were more than thirty Shino kiln sites in Gifu Prefecture, but the Mutabora kilns at Okaya produced the finest ware.

This *mizusashi*, or water container, with the *mei Kogan*, was made at Mutabora and is one of the outstanding extant Shino pieces. The body is a coarse, light egg-shell colored clay to which a thick coating of white Shino glaze, consisting mainly of feldspar, was applied.

It has the bold *yahazu-guchi* (notched) shape which was common in this period. Simple rush patterns are painted on the body with a clay called *oni-ita*, which has a high iron content. The name *Kogan* (ancient-bank) derives from this rush pattern which signifies a river bank. The bottom is flat and unglazed. The red scorch marks on the thick white glaze are called *kashoku*, or firemarks, and Shino ware with these interesting accidental effects is especially highly valued.

54

志野　芦文水指　銘古岸

Shino Ware Water Container with Rush Design
Name of Piece:　Kogan
Height:　17.8 cm.
Diameter:　18.5 cm.
Momoyama Period
Important Cultural Property
Owned by:　Mr. Kazukiyo Hatakeyama, Tokyo

鼠志野　茶碗　銘峯紅葉

11

THIS TEA bowl represents Gray or Nezumi Shino ware. The body is of a white clay, which is covered with a reddish slip. The designs are scraped out of this slip, the whole then being coated with a thick coating of the opaque, white feldspar Shino glaze.

The *mei* of the bowl is *Mine-no-Momiji* (maple on the ridge), and, along with the *Yamabana* (mountain edge) bowl owned by the Nezu Art Museum in Tokyo, it is considered one of the greatest masterpieces of Nezumi Shino.

The lower portion of the bowl, not having been covered with the reddish slip, remains white. The bottom is left unglazed.

Nezumi Shino Ware Tea Bowl
Name of Piece:　Mine-no-Momiji
Height:　8.8 cm.
Diameter:　13.8 cm.
Momoyama Period
Owned by:　Goto Art Museum, Tokyo

56

12

AMONG Shino pieces, there is a red variety called Aka-Shino, which was also made during the Momoyama Period. Extant examples are rare, and of the numerous Shino kilns in Gifu Prefecture, apparently only the Takane kiln made Aka-Shino.

The base material is the same as that of the ordinary Shino. *Oni-ita* is applied as a slip over the body and scraped off to obtain the desired designs. Shino glaze is then thinly applied and fired, thus yielding the scorched red color.

In the case of Nezumi (gray) Shino, the glaze is applied thickly.

Only two pieces of Aka-Shino with dianthus flower designs are extant; the one illustrated here is one of the masterpieces of Momoyama Shino ware. The bottom is flat and unglazed.

赤志野 撫子文小鉢

Aka-Shino Ware Plate with Dianthus Flower
  Design
Height: 4.8 cm.
Diameter: 15.5 cm.
Momoyama Period
Private Collection

13

ORIBE ware was a radically new type of pottery made in the Mino district of Gifu Prefecture during the Keicho and Genna eras (1596–1626). Its shape, design, and color varied and its vigor reflected the flamboyant taste of the Momoyama Period.

The name Oribe derives from that of the famous tea-master, FURUTA Oribe, a disciple of SEN no Rikyu, the founder of the Sen School of Tea.

Narumi Oribe, one of several varieties, uses unmixed red and white clays as a base, the two being joined together. The white clay is also used to render the designs on the red part; the white part is decorated with green glaze.

This dish is one of the outstanding pieces of Narumi Oribe and was designed for serving cake in the tea-ceremony.

It was probably made by Kagenobu, a master potter of the Motoyashiki kiln at Kujiri, Mino, which produced particularly fine ware.

60

鳴
海
織
部

手
鉢

Narumi Oribe Ware Rectangular Dish
Height: 15.5 cm.
Width and Length: 21.7 cm. × 19.5 cm.
Momoyama Period
Private Collection

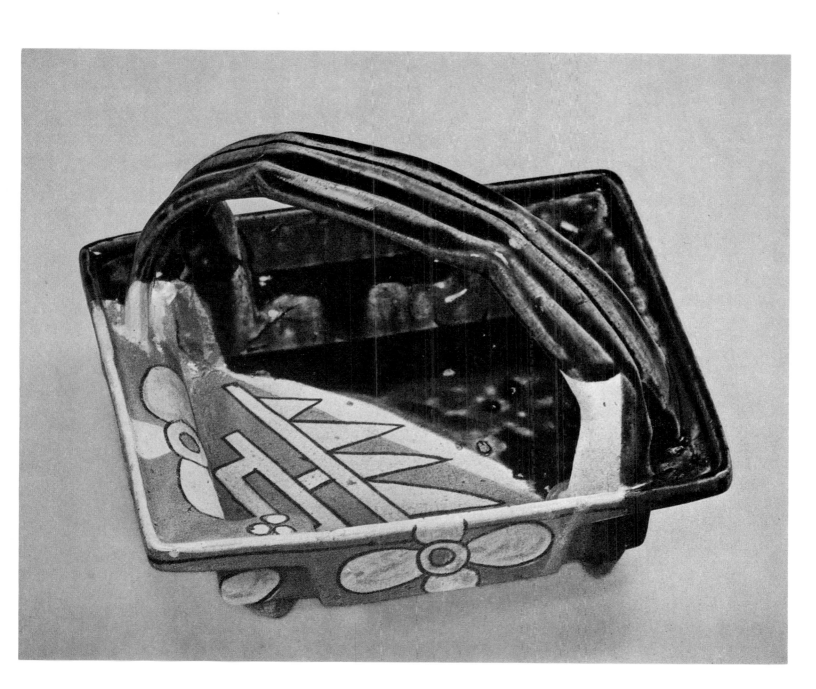

14

MANY TYPES of Oribe ware were made in the Mino district in the Keicho and Genna eras. The different varieties were named after the color, design, or place of origin; hence names such as Ao-Oribe (green), Aka-Oribe (red), Kuro-Oribe (black), E-Oribe (picture), Naruto-Oribe, Iga-Oribe, Shino-Oribe, etc. This black Oribe tea bowl has a black glaze over the entire body. This type is also referred to as *hikidashi-kuro* ("drawn-out black"), from the way it is made: the black glaze is obtained by taking the piece out of the kiln while it is still hot so that it cools very rapidly. Most of the Black Oribe ware are tea bowls, since larger objects, such as water containers or vases, were not suited to this process.

This so-called Matsukaze tea bowl, and another similar bowl owned by Koson of the Okaya family in Nagoya, are outstanding among Kuro-Oribe ware.

Its warped shape is called *kutsugata* (shoe-shape). Black glaze was coated on the inside and outside of the bowl and then partly scraped off to reveal the body. The scraped patterns are free and vigorous, and surprisingly modern in feeling. The shape and design are typical of Oribe ware.

黒織部 茶碗 銘松風

Kuro-Oribe Tea Bowl
Name of Piece: Matsukaze
Height: 6.5 cm.
Diameter: 15.7 cm.
Momoyama Period
Private Collection

62

16

RAKU-YAKI (Raku ware), a typical Japanese low-temperature glaze pottery, was first made for tea-ceremony by Chojiro during the Tensho Era (1576–80), under the guidance of SEN no Rikyu, the famous tea-master. It was considered most suited to the solemn tea-ceremony because of its soft and sober appearance. Outstanding Raku pieces were made during the Momoyama Period and the beginning of the Edo Period, but the tea bowls by Chojiro the First are especially famous for their high quality.

The *mei* or name of the piece, *Toyobo*, inscribed on the box for this tea bowl, indicates that it was an early piece made by Chojiro for a tea cultist named Toyobo. The base material is a rough-textured clay which was thickly coated with a dull black Raku glaze.

長次郎　黒楽茶碗　銘東陽坊

Kuro-Raku Tea Bowl
By:　Chojiro
Name of Piece:　Toyobo
Height:　8.5 cm.
Mouth Diameter:　12 cm.
Momoyama Period
Important Cultural Property
Private Collection

67

17

RAKU tea bowls made by Chojiro the First include famous pieces in *kuro* (black) and *aka* (red), such as the *Oguro* and *Toyobo* (black), and the *Koto, Hayafune, Muichibutsu, Tarobo,* and *Jirobo* (red). The last two named had been owned by the Konoike family, well-known collectors, but were sold at the end of World War II. The *Jirobo* is reputed to be the most beautiful of the Aka-Raku tea bowls.

The body is of red clay with a high iron content. A transparent glaze tinged with pale green has been applied. The drips of white non-transparent glaze seen at several places, are generally considered to add a certain elegance to the bowl.

There are several styles among the pieces attributed to Chojiro the First, and opinions vary as to whether he was the actual maker of all of them. Some claim that this *Jirobo* was made by Sokei, the son of SEN no Rikyu.

68

長次郎

赤楽茶碗

銘次郎坊

Aka-Raku Tea Bowl
By: Chojiro
Name of Piece: Jirobo
Height: 8.4 cm.
Mouth Diameter: 10 cm.
Momoyama Period
Private Collection

光悦

白楽片身替茶碗

銘不二山

18

KILNS making Raku ware, other than the traditional ones
of the Raku family, were called *waki-gama* (outside kilns).
Among the various *waki-gama*, Koetsu's was the most
famous. Koetsu, born into the Hon'ami family, was a
talented calligrapher and tea-master, as well as a first-rate
potter. In 1615, he set up a village of artists in Takagamine
in northern Kyoto. He had studied pottery under Jokei
and Do'nyu, second and third generations of the Raku
family, respectively.

His Raku pieces are all highly valued. This bowl, called
the *Fujisan*, which is particularly noted for its shape, is
white Raku, but the lower portion has a grayish-black glaze.

This bowl is sometimes called the *kosode*-bowl (literally, indicating a type of garment, but also suggesting a
welcomed gift) because it was specially asked for and
taken with Koetsu's daughter when she was married.

Shiro-Raku Two-Tone Tea Bowl
By: Koetsu
Name of Piece: Fujisan
Height: 8.5 cm.
Mouth Diameter: 11.6 cm.
National Treasure
Momoyama Period
Private Collection

70

19

KARATSU ware was first made by Koreans who accompanied the Japanese warriors into Japan after the Korean expeditions in the late sixteenth century. Of the more than 100 kilns founded at that time, the ones around the foot of Mt. Kishidake, near Karatsu, were the oldest; hence the name.

Karatsu is a plain, heavy, sober type of pottery, which is often considered to be the basis of modern Japanese ceramics.

This heavy, rather solemn tea bowl was made at a Mt. Kishidake kiln and is considered a masterpiece among E-Garatsu (Picture Karatsu) pottery.

The body is a coarse, grayish-white clay, which was thickly coated with a semi-translucent glaze and fired to an extremely hard state. The simple iris design was done in iron pigment.

絵唐津　菖蒲文茶碗

E-Garatsu Tea Bowl with Iris Design
Height: 9.2 cm.
Mouth Diameter: 12.2 cm.
Momoyama Period
Private Collection

20

KARATSU pottery is classified by types such as "plain," "painted," "green," "yellow," "black," "striped," "Korean," etc.

Pottery such as the water container for tea-ceremony illustrated here, covered with amber-black glaze on the upper portion and a white semi-devitrifying glaze on the lower portion, is called Chosen (Korean) Karatsu.

Chosen Karatsu includes tea bowls, water pitchers, *sake* decanters, *sake* bowls, flower vases, etc., and was produced at the Fujinokawachi kilns near Imari City, Saga Prefecture, during the Keicho era (1596–1614). It reflects the strong influence of the Oribe ware which was made in the Mino district of Gifu Prefecture during the same period.

The bottom is flat and unglazed.

朝
鮮
唐
津

水
指

Chosen Karatsu Ware Water Container
Height: 16.7 cm.
Mouth Diameter: 21 cm.
Momoyama Period
Private Collection

74

21

POTTERY made in Kagoshima Prefecture, on the southern tip of Kyushu, is usually called Satsuma ware. Its manufacture was initiated by naturalized Koreans who had been brought into the country by SHIMAZU Yoshihiro, the lord of Satsuma, after the Korean expeditions. It is said that eighteenth families forming one group landed in Kushikino and founded kilns there. Another group was led by the Korean potter Kin Kai who was ordered to set up kilns in the compounds of Yoshihiro's castle in Chosa. These kilns were later moved to Kajiki when the lord moved his castle there. Such pottery made in the castle compound of a feudal lord is called *oniwa-yaki*.

This water jar was made by Kin Kai in the Keicho era either in a Chosa or in a Kajiki kiln; it is not clear which. It is the only water jar of this type in existence.

The body is made of a blackish-brown rather fine and sticky clay with a high percentage of iron. This was coated with a subdued reddish-brown glaze, both on the inside and outside. An additional opaque white glaze was applied to the edges of the shoulders, giving this portion a luster; the mixture of white and black glaze is characteristic of Satsuma ware. The walls of the vessel are thin, and the jar is startlingly light. The bottom is flat.

古薩摩

水指

Old Satsuma Ware Water Jar
Height: 15.7 cm.
Body Diameter: 19.7 cm.
Momoyama Period
Private Collection

76

22

THE FIRST porcelain ware made in Japan is said to have been by a naturalized Korean potter named Ree San Pei at Tengudani, on the Shirakawa River, near Arita, in Hizen Province (Saga Prefecture), in 1616. Arita was then a small village in the mountains but it soon became a center of the Japanese porcelain industry.

This plate was found in the remains of the Hiekoba kiln in Arita and is believed to be a reject piece made during the early Edo Period. Early Hizen *sometsuke* (underglaze blue decoration) porcelain has become a popular collectors' item recently and numerous pieces have been found. This piece, however, is considered outstanding from the point of view of design.

The base material is a slightly gray opaque kaolin. A potted plant, the flowers of which resemble chrysanthemums and the leaves orchids, is painted with dull Chinese cobalt; the design is not supposed to represent any specific flower or plant. A white glaze, tinted slightly blue, is applied over this. The plate is warped due to over-heating.

肥前初期　染付草花文皿

Early Hizen Sometsuke Plate with Plant and
*   Flower Design*
Diameter: 14.9 cm.
Early Edo Period
Private Collection

78

23

SAKAIDA KAKIEMON (born 1596) is known the world over as the originator of Japanese *iro-e* (colored overglaze painting) porcelain. He worked as a potter under the tutelage of his father in Arita from the age of nineteen, beginning with Karatsu-type pottery and then transferring his energies to white porcelain *sometsuke*. He was financed by a prosperous merchant for the making of *iro-e* porcelain, but was unsuccessful at the beginning. He then studied under a Chinese potter in Nagasaki and after continued experiments finally succeeded in the late Kan-ei (1624–44) or early Shoho (1644–48) era. His products not only won high acclaim in Japan, but were exported even as far as Europe.

This piece with a matching cover had been exported to England, but was returned to Japan in 1961. The exact date of its manufacture is not certain, but it was certainly one of Kakiemon's early works. A similar jar, but without a cover, is designated as a National Treasure.

The base material is pure white kaolin. A thick coating of translucent glaze was applied, over which flower and bird designs were painted in red, green, blue, yellow, and black.

柿右衛門　色絵花鳥文共蓋大深鉢

Kakiemon Porcelain Jar with Chrysanthemum
   Design in Enamel Color
Height:　15.2 cm.
Diameter:　16.7 cm.
Early Edo Period
Private Collection

24

NABESHIMA porcelain was a product of the kilns belonging to the provincial lords of Nabeshima. The second generation NABESHIMA Katsushige established kilns at Iwayakawachi in 1628, and these were moved to Nangawara in 1661, and then to Okawachi in 1675, where they continued operations until the end of the Edo Period. The lords invested huge amounts of money in the hiring of potters and artists, and the best clays were used. The best Nabeshima porcelain was made during the Bunroku (1688–1704) and Kyoho (1716–1735) eras.

There are many extant pieces of Nabeshima ware with over-glaze color decoration, but this vase painted with the pine-bamboo-plum pattern is considered to be the finest. In fact, it was among the first items to be designated "Important Cultural Property" when the system was instituted by the government in 1935.

The other side has a chrysanthemum-orange design, crane and turtle paintings decorating the lower portion. The bottom has a shallow indentation.

色鍋島　松竹梅文瓶

Iro-Nabeshima Porcelain Vase with Pine-Bamboo-Plum
    Design
Height: 30.6 cm.
Important Cultural Property
Middle Edo Period
Private Collection

25

KUTANI ware was first made by GOTO Saijiro on order of his lord, MAEDA Toshiharu, at Kutani, Ishikawa Prefecture. Dates are uncertain, but the first kiln which produced so-called Old Kutani was established around 1655, and fell into disuse, probably in the 1690's.

There are *sometsuke* among old Kutani ware, but *iro-e* Kutani is the most famous type. Large Old Kutani plates were the most treasured, although other objects were also made.

The base material is grayish white kaolin, which has a low refraction and therefore often becomes distorted in shape. The whole inner surface is decorated with paintings of myna birds, bamboo, flowers, rocks, and withered stems, in green, blue, yellow, red, and black. The back of the plate is decorated with a vigorous pine-bamboo-plum design.

84

古九谷 色絵叭々鳥文大皿

*Large Old Kutani Porcelain Plate with
    Myna Bird Pattern*
Height: 8.3 cm.
Mouth Diameter: 42.4 cm.
Important Cultural Property
Early Edo Period
Owned by: Tokyo National Museum

26

OLD KUTANI ware, decorated primarily with green and yellow over-glaze colors, is called Ao-Kutani (literally, "Green Kutani").

The clay, the quality of the glaze, and especially the designs of Ao-Kutani pieces made prior to the Genroku era (1688–1703) are quite different from those of other types of Old Kutani ware.

The ware is noted for its fresh, bold designs, and the one on this large plate is strikingly at variance, in both motif and design, with anything one might expect from an acquaintanceship with ordinary Japanese painting or decorative art. An old tree is rendered in green, yellow, and black against a yellow and black wave-patterned background; and on the broad edge of the plate is a pattern resembling wood grain.

There are a number of different motifs which appear in designs on Ao-Kutani wares, but they are all original and striking, and are all accomplished without the use of red.

Of the numerous extant Ao-Kutani pieces, this plate is considered one of the most beautiful. It was formerly owned by the Nagao Art Museum, Kanagawa Prefecture.

青九谷　樹木文皿

Ao-Kutani Plate with Tree Design
Height: 10 cm.
Diameter: 4.5 cm.
Edo Period
Private Collection

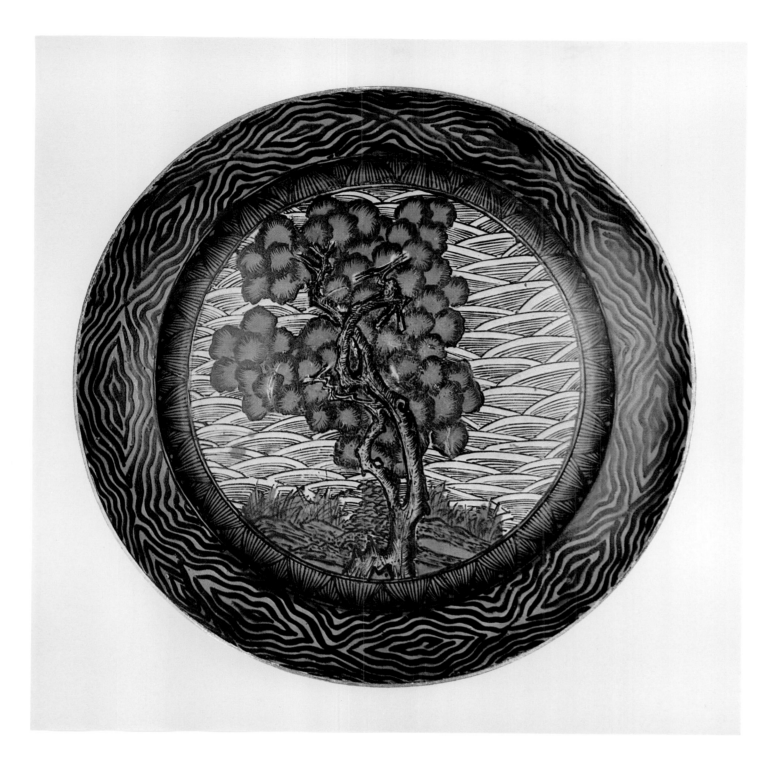

27

KYOTO was an old pottery center. In its kilns, Sue ware of the Tumulus Period, green-glaze pottery of the Heian Period, the traditional Kawarake (unglazed earthenware), and Raku-ware of the Momoyama Period had been produced. Also, kilns around Kiyomizu, Otowa and Mizoro-ike, all in Kyoto, flourished during the Edo Period. But the man who really established Kyoto as a great center of pottery, and incidentally exerted considerable influence over other kilns, was Ninsei.

He employed various styles and many of his masterpieces are extant. Of these, perhaps this jar is the foremost; at any rate, it fetched a fabulous price when it was sold.

The shape imitates that of the so-called "Luzon jars" imported into Japan during the Momoyama and early Edo Periods. Its body is of light-weight, egg-shell colored clay. The entire surface of the jar was coated with an opaque white glaze which has cracked polygonally. The colors employed include gold and silver, as well as dark red, green, and purple.

The bottom is flat and has the inscription "Ninsei."

仁清 色絵藤花文茶壺

Iro-e Wisteria Pattern Tea Jar
By: Ninsei
Height: 29.2 cm.
Body Diameter: 27.3 cm.
Early Edo Period
National Treasure
Owned by: Hakone Art Museum, Shizuoka Prefecture

88

28

KENZAN, the younger brother of the famous painter, OGATA Korin, was born in 1663. In 1689, he established a kiln in Narutaki, where he made pottery for about 23 years and then moved successively to another part of Kyoto, Edo (Tokyo), and finally to Sano in Tochigi Prefecture. He spent most of his later years engaged in painting and calligraphy rather than pottery, except for the brief period in Sano.

This piece was a product of his Narutaki days. The body is a light brown clay. White translucent glaze was applied, after which it was fired at a high-temperature. The plum flower is painted in red, green, and yellow. Kenzan showed a particular preference for this *yariume* (spear-stemmed plum); it is executed with the rounded brushstrokes characteristic of his calligraphy.

The name "Kenzan" is inscribed in *sometsuke* on the base of the bowl.

乾
山

色
絵
槍
梅
文
茶
碗

*Tea Bowl with Spear-stemmed Plum Pattern
   in Color*
By: Kenzan
Height: 9.9 cm.
Mouth Diameter: 10.2 cm.
Middle Edo Period
Private Collection

90

29

THE OUTSTANDING feature of Kenzan porcelain is its *etsuke,* or painting. This plate was made while Kenzan was still in Kyoto and is one of a set of plates, each with different designs.

The body, a coarse clay with a high percentage of iron, was covered with a white slip. After an opaque glaze had been applied, it was fired at a high temperature before the painting was done. The cedar woods are depicted freely and are typical of Kenzan's painting.

His name is inscribed on the bottom.

乾山　色絵杉林文皿

Iro-e Cedar-Wood Pattern Plate
By: Kenzan
Height: 2.2 cm.
Mouth Diameter: 16.3 cm.
Middle Edo Period
Private Collection

金
工

Metal Work

30

THE HISTORY of metal work in Japan begins in the Yayoi Period which lasted from about 300 B.C. to 200-300 A.D. Apart from the importation of swords, mirrors, etc., from China, bronze objects were first cast in the northern part of Kyushu, the southernmost island of Japan. Later in the period, with the advance of bronze and iron casting techniques, the center of production moved to the Kinki area.

The *dotaku* are objects peculiar to this period. The fact that these objects are not seen among relics of the following Tumulus Period is difficult to explain historically. They are similar in shape to the bronze bells of ancient China, but whether *dotaku* originated there is not clear. The fact that a number of clappers were found in conjunction with the more than 300 bells excavated in the Kinki area, leads us to believe that these objects originally were musical instruments. Very likely they assumed a symbolic or religious significance with the passage of time.

The pictured *dotaku* is typical, with running water designs cast on its sides. It is thickly cast of high quality bronze containing a large percentage of tin. The perforations on the upper part are thought to be traces of *katamochi*, supports to hold the inner and outer molds together.

This piece was unearthed in Hyogo Prefecture.

流水文銅鐸

Dotaku Decorated with Running Water Motif
Bronze
Height : 45 cm.
Yayoi Period
Important Cultural Property
Owned by : Tokyo National Museum

96

31

DURING the Yayoi Period, bronze was introduced into Japan from the continent, and casting techniques were eventually learned and developed.

The *dotaku* were cast in sand or stone molds. The cross-section view of the body is spindle-shaped and the arc on the upper part was probably used to hang it like a bell.

They are distinguished by the decorative designs; this one is called the *kesagake dotaku* because of its "surplice" pattern reliefs by which the sides of the bell are divided into six sections each, making space for 12 relief line drawings. The expression is primitive, but vividly illustrates the life of the period. On the upper right of one side there is a spider and a praying mantis; on the upper left a dragonfly; on the middle right a crane-like bird picking at a fish; on the middle left a turtle eating fish; on the lower right a hunting scene with five dogs surrounding a wild boar and a man getting ready to shoot an arrow; and on the lower left a turtle and other reptile-like creatures. On the pictured side, the upper right illustrates a dragonfly; the upper left reptile-like creatures; the middle right a hunter prepared to shoot a deer; the middle left a woman weaving; the lower right a gabled and high floored building; and the lower left two people pounding rice. This piece is said to have been excavated in Kagawa Prefecture, Shikoku.

98

袈裟襷文銅鐸

Dotaku Decorated with "Surplice" Pattern
Bronze
Height: 42.7 cm.
Yayoi Period
National Treasure
Owned by: Mr. Hachiro Ohashi, Tokyo

99

32

DURING the earlier half of the Kofun or Tumulus Period, which lasted for about 300 years immediately after the Yayoi Period, numerous Chinese bronze mirrors were imported and eventually they were cast in Japan in imitation of the Chinese models. Production of mirrors in China dates back to about 770 B.C. Most of these mirrors were cast in bronze and had a relief pattern on the back, though there are also some silver, iron, and lead mirrors, which are, however, exceptional and very scarce.

The patterns of the *daryu* on this mirror, as do the designs on other mirrors manufactured by the mirror-making clan (*kagami-tsukuri-be*), show a departure from those of the Chinese original. The casting technique is superb, even details being finely executed, indicating the marked development which the art had undergone.

The site of excavation of this mirror is not known.

鼉
龍
鏡

Daryu (crocodile-dragon) Mirror
Bronze
Diameter: 38.5 cm.
Tumulus Period
Important Cultural Property
Owned by: Tokyo National Museum

33

METAL WORK gradually began to flourish during this period, as specialized clans such as the *kagami-tsukuri-be* (mirror makers), *yamato-kaji-be* (swordsmiths), *kara-kaji-be* (bronze makers), etc., were established. Relics from this period include bronze mirrors, swords, armor, harnessry, and other accessories. These were first made in imitation of imported Chinese goods, but gradually one can see the emergence of an indigenous style.

The geometrical pattern of this mirror is radically different from the ones on Chinese mirrors. It is a variation on a pattern called *chokko-mon* which can be seen on the deer hornwork and the stone coffins of the same period. This pattern, the *chokko-mon*, consists of simple straight and curved lines surrounding a cross. The pictured mirror has a plain center which is divided into four sections with *chokko-mon* variants encircling it, the outermost of the four being further divided into eight rings with another set of *chokko-mon* variants.

This mirror, unlike the Chinese mirrors, is devoid of illustrations of complex thoughts or myths. Instead, it presents us with a fresh and simple geometric design.

直弧文鏡

Chokko-mon Mirror
Bronze
Diameter: 28 cm.
Tumulus Period
Owned by: Imperial Household

102

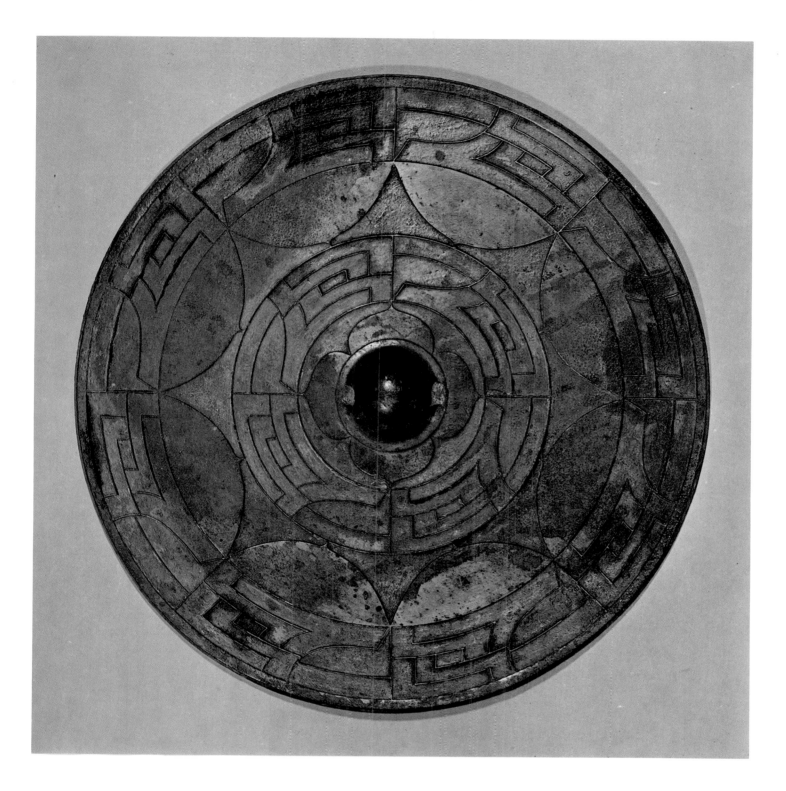

34

THE HELMETS of the ancient period and those used by the *samurai* from the twelfth century differ significantly in shape as well as in construction. The ancient helmets have no uniquely Japanese features. Rather, they resemble those of China and even Western he'mets.

There were two types of helmet in the Tumulus Period, one being this visored type and the other having a prow-shaped front. Though helmets intended for practical use were of iron, this one, perhaps more ornamental than practical, is made of two thin sheets of gilt bronze attached together with decorat ve rivets. The visor in front is rendered in arabesque-type openwork and the receptacle on the round top may originally have held ornamental plumes.

Noteworthy are the fish and animal engravings done in a primitive but humorous dotted line technique. It is a type of engraving seen in other ancient relics, but this is the only extant helmet with such designs, which may have had some religious significance in addition to their ornamental function.

Iron helmets buried in earth tend to corrode and lose their original shape. This helmet, being gilt bronze, is well preserved and thus is a particularly valuable example.

眉庇付冑

Visored Helmet
Gilt Bronze
Height: 21 cm.
Tumulus Period
Owned by: Tokyo National Museum

104

35

WITH THE introduction of Buddhism in 538, all aspects of Japanese culture were energized. The production of Buddhist statues and related objects was begun by artisans who came from the Asiatic mainland. In the field of metal work, temple decorations, nimbi of Buddhist statues, and other ornamental objects were produced.

Ban, or banners, are usually made out of fabric and such a *ban* as this, made of gilt bronze, is very unusual, though similar ones are known to have been made in China during the T'ang Dynasty.

This *ban* is of sheet bronze cut in arabesque-type openwork, heavily gilt and then finished with line engravings on both sides, the patterns on the two sides being mirror images of each other. Seven pieces of the same sized *ban* and one slightly longer piece are hinged together lengthwise. Figures, such as a seated Buddha and an angel, a lion and an angel, etc., are done in openwork and line engraving. Around these main patterns are designs of honeysuckle in arabesque style, which seem to have been popular in that period.

Remains of red and green coloring can be seen in the eyes, mouth, hair, and part of the pedestal, indicating that the *ban* was originally colored. Also, at the end of the row there is some red thread, which would suggest that this end was ornamented with red silk cloth.

金銅小幡

Small Ban or Banner
Gilt Bronze
Length: 40.5 cm.
Suiko Period
Important Cultural Property
Owned by: Tokyo National Museum

36

DURING THE early Nara (Hakuho) Period, Buddhist culture prospered and numerous temples were built. In connection with this construction, the manufacture of Buddhist statues was carried out on a large scale and wax mold casting methods were developed. We have, aside from sculpture, only a few relics of Hakuho metal work, but the reliquaries shown here are excellent representatives of the art of this short period.

They were discovered inside the foundation stone of a pagoda in the remains of Shufukuji monastery in Shiga Prefecture. Three *shari* (*shari* or *sarira* are relics of Gautama Buddha or stones with equivalent significance) are kept in the glass urn with a solid gold cover. This urn is kept in the inner gold casket, which in turn is placed in the silver casket. A gilt bronze box holds this silver casket. Perhaps the whole system of boxes was put into a wooden box and buried.

The gold and silver containers are of hammered metal sheets. The lids are held with *hoshu* (flame-topped ball) headed nails from both sides. Inside the golden inner casket is an openwork octafoil lotus pedestal to hold the glass urn in place in the center. The gilt bronze outer casket was cast together with the pedestal. Here too the lid is held with *hoshu* headed nails from both sides.

The practice of the preservation of *shari* in glass containers kept in gold, silver, and gilt bronze reliquaries is also apparent from objects found in the foundation stone of the five-storied pagoda of the Horyuji monastery.

舍利容器

Shari Reliquaries

Glass Urn	*Height:*	*3*	*cm.*
Golden Inner Casket	*Width:*	*6.1*	*cm.*
	Length:	*4.3*	*cm.*
	Height:	*3.3*	*cm.*
Silver Inner Casket	*Width:*	*7.9*	*cm.*
	Length:	*5.8*	*cm.*
	Height:	*4*	*cm.*
Gilt Bronze Outer Casket	*Width:*	*10.6*	*cm.*
	Length:	*7.9*	*cm.*
	Height:	*7.6*	*cm.*

Hakuho Period
National Treasure
Owned by: Omi Jingu Shrine, Shiga Prefecture

108

37

THE EMPEROR Shomu, who ruled during the mid-Nara (Tempyo) Period, was an ardent worshiper of Buddha, and during his reign there were frequent missions to China. Buddhist culture reached its peak in this era, which also saw great progress in metal working techniques. The majority of the art objects in the Shosoin today belonged to Todaiji, a large Buddhist temple complex built during this period. Temples like those of Todaiji and Horyuji required various Buddhist ornamental objects, all of which show the influence of T'ang Dynasty art in their shapes and casting techniques.

Buddhist influence gave rise to the custom of cremating the dead, the first recorded instance in Japan being the cremation of a priest in 700 A.D. The vessels for the ashes were made of several materials—wood, clay, metal, glass, etc.

This urn, very likely intended as a funeral urn, is round, thickly cast in bronze, and has a flat cover with a *hoshu* (flame-topped ball) to secure a string. It was finished with a hand lathe after casting and then gilt thickly with gold amalgam. Because of this thick gilding, it is still quite brilliant, in contrast to the usual green patina of bronze.

There is no epitaph indicating whose urn it was. It was excavated in Kamori, Taima Village, Katakatsuragi County, Nara.

金銅骨壺

Funeral Urn
Gilt Bronze
Height: 18.7 cm.
Nara Period
Owned by: Tokyo National Museum

110

38

THE DECORATIVE patterns of art works made in the Nara Period generally imitated those of T'ang Dynasty Chinese objects. *Hosoge* (floral arabesque) patterns and *toka* (Chinese floral) patterns can be seen on numerous art objects made during this period. Animal motifs commonly employed included the *hoo* (Chinese phoenix), lion, deer, etc., as well as hunting scenes. The patterns rendered on this water container are typical examples.

This gilt bronze *suiteki*, a container to hold water for making ink, which originally belonged to the Horyuji monastery, was later offered to the Imperial Household, and was finally transferred to the Tokyo National Museum. It is part of a set including a gilt bronze *bokusho* (ink-stick stand) and three spoons, with willow, lotus, and gourd shapes, respectively. The oldest *suiteki* extant in Japan, it has a narrow mouth, swells towards the lower part of the body, and is supported by three short legs. The swelling part of the body is divided into three sections by encircling floral designs. The center of each section depicts a Chinese phoenix with outspread wings surrounded by floral-leaf designs rendered in *kebori* (hair-line engraving). The ground area is covered with *nanako* (fish roe) or dense dotted designs in relief.

Chinese floral pattern engravings are rendered on the cover, which supports a ball-shaped knob.

水
滴

匙

墨
床

Suiteki (Small Water Container)
Gilt Bronze
Height: 7.3 cm.
Body Diameter: 8.2 cm.
Nara Period
Important Cultural Property
Owned by: Tokyo National Museum

39

THERE ARE numerous metal objects in the Shosoin Repository, including weapons, harnessry, ornamental objects related to Buddhist rituals, personal accessories, interior decorations, utensils, ornamental furniture, playthings, and mirrors. Casting, wrought iron work, chasing, inlaying, plating, and hand lathe work techniques are all to be found. The most commonly used materials were copper, silver, and gold.

About a hundred swords belonging to this short type are preserved in the Repository. More accessories than weapons, they were hung from a leather belt by cords. The illustrated sword was offered to the Great Buddha of Nara by Lady Tachibana, the consort of Emperor Shomu, as is noted by the inscription on a wooden tag attached to it. The handle is of rhinocerous horn and the scabbard is of wood covered entirely with silver arabesque openwork, in which green glass beads and small white pearls have been inlaid. The openwork of this period differs from that of the Suiko Period in that it is not evenly flat, but molded to give an impression of solidity. The same arabesque-style openwork is applied to the silver and gold ornaments on the tip of the handle. The blade of the sword, although short, is extremely well tempered.

刀
子

Tosu (short sword)
Length: 22.9 cm.
Nara Period
Preserved in: Shosoin Repository, Nara

114

40

THE ART of the Heian Period, apparently influenced by the luxurious life of the ruling Fujiwara family, has a color and elegance of its own. Naturally, the Heian metal work exhibits these qualities too. Even the solemn Buddhist altar objects reflect this delicate and elegant Heian aesthetic.

The shape of this sutra box, its crenellations, and the fittings on the cover all testify to its origin in Fujiwara times. But the designs are perhaps the most sensitive reflection of the age.

It was found in a cast bronze case, together with other objects, such as crystal beads and pieces of wood, at the site of the Nyohodo Temple on Mt. Hiei. It contained copies of the Lotus Sutra reputedly transcribed by Lady Jotomonin, consort of Emperor Ichijo.

Both body and cover are plated with silver and engraved with *hosoge* patterns (a stylized floral design based ultimately on Indian prototypes). In the center of the cover is an inscription of five characters. The engraved characters and designs are gilded.

金銅経箱

Gilt Bronze Sutra Box
Height: 8.3 cm.
Length: 28.7 cm.
Fujiwara Period
National Treasure
Owned by: Enryakuji Monastery, Hiei-zan, Shiga
Prefecture

116

41

METAL WORK centered on Buddhist altar fittings thrived during the ujiwara Period also. However, with the introduction and growing popularity of esoteric, specifically Tendai, Buddhism, the fear that in the declining days of the Buddha sutras might be destroyed, led to their burial in *kyozuka*, or sutra mounds, and thus to a new type of metal object.

This *hoto*, or sacred miniature tower, one of the best of its kind, was excavated from a sutra mound near the main hall of the Kuramadera. Several cylindrical sutra cases, Buddhist images, altar pieces, and bronze mirrors were found at the same site. Sacred towers used to bury *shari* relics also became popular from this period.

One of the bronze cylindrical cases mentioned above bears an inscription with the date of Hoan Gannen, corresponding to the year 1120, which can thus be viewed as the probable approximate time of production of this tower too.

Cast in bronze, it is composed of three sections, a square altar, cylindrical body, and roof. The cylindrical body is inserted in a circular groove carved on the upper surface of the square altar and is hollow to permit storage of sutras. The lower portion of the body is encircled by a double-petal lotus pedestal. The opening on the upper part of the body is narrow and the roof is fitted on like a lid. The roof itself is hipped (*shichu-zukuri*) with a *hoshu* at the center. Fine details of tiles decorate the slopes of the roof, the eaves being realistically fashioned and a well shaped wind bell is appropriately hung.

The tower, having been excavated from the earth, bears a green patina.

銅宝塔

Bronze Hoto or Sacred Miniature Tower
Height: 57.9 cm.
Fujiwara Period
National Treasure
Owned by: Kuramadera Monastery, Kyoto

118

42

WORKMANSHIP on sword mountings originally was directed to the purposes of protecting the blade and preventing danger to the wielder. Later, two types of swords were developed, one for use in battle, and the other for decorative and ceremonial purposes. The workmanship on swords preserved in the Shosoin, made in the Nara Period, serves both purposes. After the Heian Period, there was a clear distinction between the two types, the blades of the decorative ceremonial swords merely serving to suggest the shape of the sword. This was the case up through the Muromachi Period, but after the Momoyama Period, even ceremonial swords for the *samurai* were made with real blades.

This is a typical decorative Japanese ceremonial sword for Imperial Court officials. And it shows a considerable departure from the gold and silver inlaid Chinese-type sword mountings seen in the Shosoin Repository.

The scabbard is coated with aventurine lacquer with long-tailed cock designs done in inlaid mother-of-pearl. The handle is covered with white sharkskin. The sword guard and other metal pieces are of gilt bronze with chrysanthemum branch designs done in high relief. The decorative rivets seem to have had colored glass fittings, but these have been lost and, furthermore, some of the rivets themselves have been replaced. The blade of the sword is of wood.

This sword is said to have been used by FUJIWARA Kamatari, but actually it was made only in the latter part of the Heian Period.

尾長鳥螺鈿文飾大刀

*Decorative Sword with Long-Tailed Cock in Raden
    (Mother-of-Pearl Work) on the Scabbard*
Length: 103.7 cm.
Fujiwara Period
National Treasure
Owned by: Tokyo National Museum

120

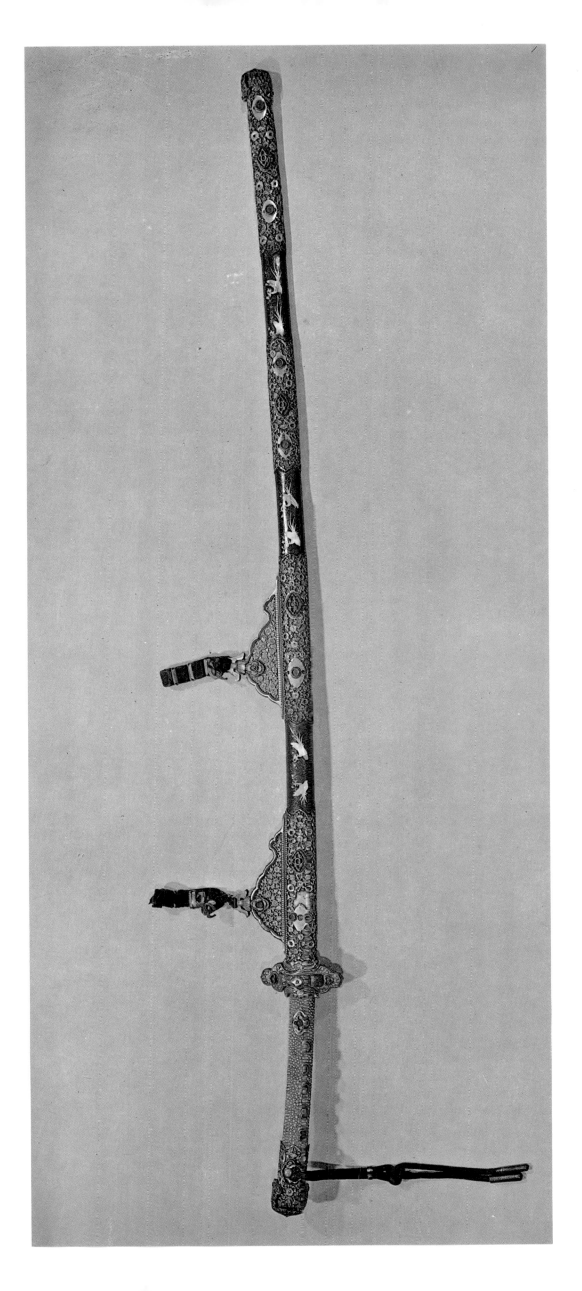

羽
黒
鏡

43

Mirrors Excavated from Haguro

METAL WORK of the Fujiwara Period, excluding Buddhist altar objects, consisted mainly of mirrors, swords, and other armor. Mirrors were made continuously from the Tumulus Period through the Edo Period, and therefore can be used as an indication of the changes in metal work style and to gauge the standard of handicrafts in general in the different periods.

These mirrors were excavated from a pond in front of Haguro Shrine, located on Mt. Haguro in Yamagata Prefecture in Northern Japan, into which they had been thrown by believers as offerings. Several hundred pieces have been recovered and many times that number are believed to be still buried in the pond.

Mirrors were originally imported into Japan from China. Purely Japanese-style mirrors were made from the eleventh century, the style reaching its peak in the twelfth century. Its chief characteristics are the thinness of the mirror and the high, thin encircling edges. The patterns on the back were made by skillful pallet work (applied to the surface of the clay molds). Natural subjects, such as plants, birds, and butterflies, are elegantly portrayed. These four are representative mirrors of the period.

1) Two water fowls just rising to fly are shown on the sides of the twisted chrysanthemum knob, with grass on the bank rendered on the lower portion and the outspread branches of a tree on the upper part.

1) Mirror with Flower and Water-fowl Design
Diameter: 10.2 cm.
Fujiwara Period
Owned by: Tokyo National Museum

2) Bamboo fences with grass designs at the bases are rendered on the upper and lower portions with two flying birds and a butterfly in between, with a simple knob at the center. Balanced designs on the upper and lower portions are rather rare in mirrors of this period.

2) Mirror with Design of Bamboo Fence and Two Birds
Diameter: 10.5 cm.
Fujiwara Period
Owned by: Tokyo National Museum

3) A design of yellow roses in full bloom, two birds, and two butterflies are distributed around the knob.

3) Mirror with Yellow Rose, Birds, and Butterfly Design
Diameter: 10.8 cm.
Fujiwara Period
Owned by: Tokyo National Museum

4) The pine and crane combination is a popular Japanese motif. Two cranes and pine leaves are depicted revolving around the twisted chrysanthemum knob in the center.

4) Mirror with Pine and Crane Design
Diameter: 10.5 cm.
Fujiwara Period
Owned by: Tokyo National Museum

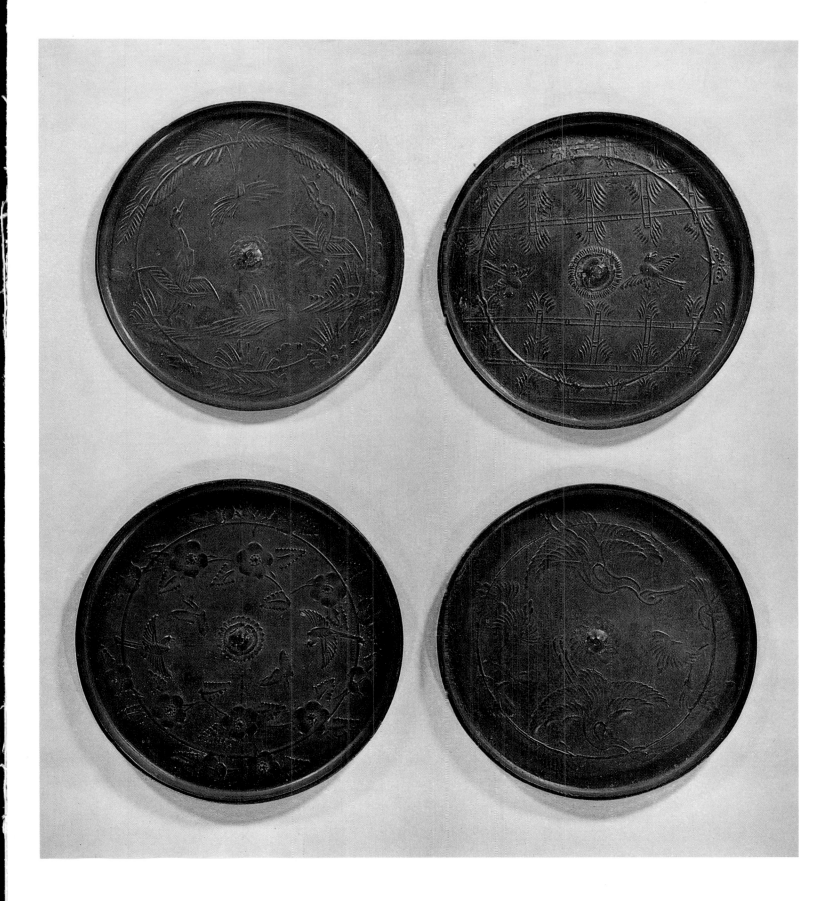

44

JAPANESE mirrors attained a high artistic level in the
Kamakura Period. In addition, they became larger and
thicker as compared with those of the Heian Period. The
workmanship of the designs on the back of the mirrors
also marked a change from the previous era. The Heian
Period patterns, while using natural motifs—flowers, trees,
birds, butterflies, etc.—somehow seem removed from the
actual world. The Kamakura patterns and compositions
are more earthy and naturalistic.

This mirror, depicting a great plum tree in full bloom
with outspread branches over a chrysanthemum patterned
fence and a flock of sparrows, is reminiscent of Japanese
painting. The designs are done in higher relief than those
of the previous period. Similar patterns can be seen in a
few other mirrors of this age, attesting to its popularity.
But the workmanship and casting technique of this particular piece are unparalleled.

檜垣梅樹飛雀鏡

Mirror with Fence, Plum Tree, and Sparrow Designs
Bronze
Diameter: 19.1 cm.
Kamakura Period
Important Cultural Property
Owned by: Nukisaki Shrine, Gumma Prefecture

124

45

THE ELEGANT art of the Heian Period, which was a product of the culture of the aristocracy, gradually gave way to the solemn and vigorous *samurai* culture of the Kamakura Period. However, objects in the tradition of Fujiwara court art were still made, and a number of them are extant in temples and shrines in the Kinki area. This silver nimbus is one such item.

Gilt bronze Buddhist images with gilt bronze halos done in delicate openwork had been made all through the Asuka Period and this piece is in the same tradition. It was probably attached to a silver Buddha, which has since been lost.

The boat-shaped nimbus was carved from silver sheets in openwork and then silver plated. The halo, which was behind the head of the figure (*zuko*), has the shape of an eight-lobed lotus flower. The nimbus encircling the body (*kyoshinko*) has *hosoge* done in openwork. Buddhist images in vermilion and green are painted in the 13 circles, which are inlaid with thin sheets of crystal.

銀光背

Silver Nimbus
Height: 23.5 cm.
Kamakura Period
National Treasure
Owned by: Shitennoji Monastery, Osaka

126

46

ESOTERIC BUDDHISM was introduced to Japan at the beginning of the Heian Period, and altar objects were brought into the country at the same time. Later, a great number of these were made domestically, the workmanship reaching its peak in the early Kamakura Period.

The elaborate ceremonies of esoteric Buddhism required a great number of objects, but this five piece set represents the main types. An outstanding example of esoteric Buddhist art, legend has it that it was offered to the Itsukushima Shrine by the Taira family in the late Heian Period. But, judging from the style of workmanship, it seems more likely that the five pieces were made in the early Kamakura Period.

The four-lobed *Kongoban* is supported on "animal" legs with *shikami* or lion-head ornaments. It has a lotus pedestal in the middle, done in high relief, on which the *Gokorei* is placed. The grips of the four pieces are done in the same pattern—encircling *kimen* (ogre face) designs in the middle and lotus motifs on both ends. *Shikami* designs are also applied to the base of the *ko*, or prongs. The bell portion of the *Gokorei* is heavily ornamented with arabesques and there are inscriptions in Sanskrit on four sides.

金銅密教法具

Esoteric Buddhist Altar Objects
Gilt Bronze

Kongoban (Vajra stand)	*Length:*	*21.8 cm.*
	Width:	*28.6 cm.*
	Height:	*6.2 cm.*
Gokorei (5-pronged Vajra-bell)	*Length:*	*20.9 cm.*
	Diameter:	*9 cm.*
Dokkosho (Vajra)	*Length:*	*18.5 cm.*
Sankosho (3-pronged Vajra)	*Length:*	*18.8 cm.*
Gokosho (5-pronged Vajra)	*Length:*	*19 cm.*

Kamakura Period
National Treasure
Owned by: Itsukushima Shrine, Hiroshima

128

47

IN THE KAMAKURA Period there emerged a new movement in Buddhism, which involved a faith in relics and thus brought about a prolific production of reliquaries. Several are to be found in Saidaiji, Kairyuji, and other Nara monasteries. The one shown here is perhaps the most splendid. It is of gilt bronze, shaped like a lantern, and contains a relic urn inside. The hexagonal petal-shaped roof of the stupa is topped with a *hoshu* (flame-topped ball) and is divided into four circular sections. *Nanako* are rendered on the ground, with dragons, clouds, and lotus arabesque patterns in low relief. At the edges of the petals are *warabi-te*, or hooks, from which wind bells and various ornaments are hung.

The body of the reliquary is divided into six panels. The upper part is done in arabesque openwork, and glass ornaments are hung in a loose network. The center part is richly decorated with chrysanthemum, peony, dragon, lotus, and gentian patterns done in openwork and relief. The lower portion has high relief and openwork lion and peony patterns. The portion just above the base is done in low relief floral designs with *hoshu*.

A small Buddha Dainichi is attached to the cover of the urn, with a roof-like awning supported by four legs. Sacred relics of Buddha are thought to have been contained in this urn.

This masterpiece of the Kamakura Period is said to have belonged to the Priest Eison, who is credited with having restored Saidaiji to its ancient grandeur.

舎
利
塔

Lantern-shaped Reliquary
Gilt Bronze
Total Height: 37 cm.
Body Height: 18.2 cm.
Kamakura Period
National Treasure
Owned by: Saidaiji Monastery, Nara

130

48

SUCH FLORAL baskets served as containers for lotus flowers strewn during the Buddhist rites of "flower strewing" at memorial services in temples. The practice dated from the Nara Period and there are 800 bamboo baskets preserved in the Shosoin.

Other metal baskets were made, but this particular one is of gilt bronze partially plated with silver. Bronze sheets were cut in round platter-like shapes and ornamental borders were attached. Arabesques (*hosoge*) were carved in low relief and in openwork. The entire body was gilded and the flower portions of the pattern were further silver plated. A delicate technique combining low relief with accents done in *suki-bori* (high relief engraving) was employed. The mixture of gold and silver is frequently seen in works of the late Heian and Kamakura Periods.

Rings are attached at three places under the platter for cords, by which the basket was hung, and gilt bronze, octagonal pyramid-shaped metal fittings are attached to the ends of the cords.

132

宝相華透彫華籠

Hosoge Pattern Openwork Floral Basket Used for
    Buddhist Rites
Gilt Bronze Partly Silver Plated
Diameter: 28.8 cm.
Kamakura Period
National Treasure
Owned by: Shinshoji Monastery, Shiga Prefecture

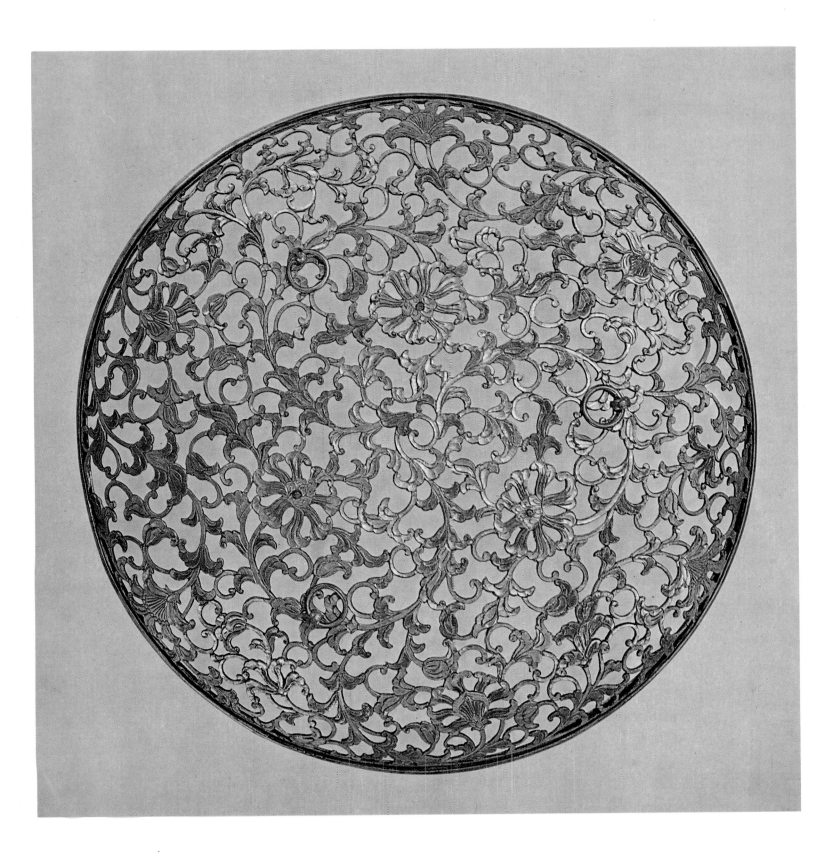

49

ARMOR WORN in Japan from the Tumulus Period through the Nara Period more or less imitated that used on the Asiatic mainland. However, with the rise of a local *samurai* class in the Heian Period, a distinctly Japanese style was gradually developed. Understandably, the form of the armor changed with the type of warfare conducted. Characteristic of Japanese armor are its decorative shape and workmanship. Armor-making involved not only metal work, but also lacquer art, textiles, and a number of other handicrafts. It was therefore one of the most representative art forms of the *samurai* culture.

O-yoroi (great armor), also called the *shikisho-no-yoroi* or *kisenaga-yoroi*, was generally worn by military leaders in mounted archery warfare. Japanese armor, as made in the Heian Period, underwent very little change in the following Kamakura Period.

This armor was made in late Kamakura, and emphasis was more on its decorative aspects than on its practicability as a defensive armor. It is reputed to have been offered to the Kushibiki Hachiman Shrine by the Nambu family, powerful in northern Japan.

It consists of a helmet, *do* (body armor with the right side left open), *waidate* (armor for the right side under the arm), *osode* (shoulder piece), *sendan-no-ita* (guard to protect the bared portion of the right front shoulder) and *kyubi-noita* (guard for the left front shoulder). These portions, with the exception of the helmet, are made of *kozane*, small plates of iron, backed with leather and lacquered black, which are threaded together with red braid; *akaito-odoshi* means threading with red braid. Gilt fittings with double chrysanthemum reliefs ornament various rivetted points of the armor as well as the *hachimanza* (crown of the helmet). The *osode* is ornamented with metal work designs of chrysanthemums over a fence with clouds overhead and the character for "one."

赤糸縅鎧

Akaito-odoshi Armor
Body armor height: 33.3 cm.
Osode Length: 36.4 cm.
Kamakura Period
National Treasure
Owned by: Kushibiki Hachiman Shrine, Aomori
Prefecture

134

50

THE *domaru*, or cuirass, is a more abbreviated form of armor than the *o-yoroi*, and was worn by the foot-soldier. It closely resembles the *keiko* (armor with thin iron plates threaded together) worn in the ancient period. As mounted archery warfare gave way to dismounted fighting in Kamakura times, the *domaru* gained in popularity.

There is a single continuous piece tied together at the right side. The lower part is divided into eight pieces, allowing considerable freedom of movement. Instead of a *senda-no-ita* and *kyubi-no-ita* to protect the shoulders, the *gyoyo* (shoulder guard) is suspended from the shoulders over the breast. The old type *domaru* did not have a helmet nor *osode*, but from the latter part of the Kamakura Period it was supplemented with the *suji-kabuto* helmet and *osode*.

This armor is representative of the *domaru* of the late Kamakura Period. *Kozane* are threaded together with *kashitori-ito* (mixed colored threads, suggesting the wings of a jay), except for the shoulder and breast, which are done in red braid. The helmet is lacquered black with 32 lines radiating from the crown and is ornamented with a large *kuwagata*. The bases of the *kuwagata* and other metal fittings are covered with *nanako* (fish roe), or dense small dots in relief, and decorated with *gosan-no-kiri* (five and three paulownia crest) patterns.

This armor was made in the early Muromachi Period, and is still in perfect condition.

樫鳥糸縅肩赤銅丸

Kashitori-ito-odoshi Aka-domaru Armor
Body Armor Height: 64.4 cm.
Osode Length: 46.2 cm.
Muromachi Period
Important Cultural Property
Owned by: Mr. Kazusuke Akita, Tokyo

136

51

THE OLDEST hanging lantern known in Japan is preserved at the Itsukushima Shrine: it bears an inscription of the Shohei reign period (1366), and is simple in shape with little decoration. There were lanterns made from the early Muromachi Period in cast and wrought bronze which were outstanding in technique and workmanship. The lanterns became larger and openwork in bronze sheets became popular in the following Momoyama and Edo Periods, but the workmanship did not show any significant advance.

This lantern was excavated in almost perfect condition, except for a hanging ring which was missing, in the compound of Chiba monastery in Chiba City. There is a date inscribed on the headpiece which corresponds to 1550.

The walls of the hexagonal light chamber (*hibukuro*) are done in openwork plum and bamboo designs. With the exception of the door of this compartment, the whole object, including the headpiece and legs, is cast in one piece. The caster was probably a skilled craftsman attached to the Sano Temmyo group in Tochigi Prefecture.

The headpiece, with a *hoshu* knob in the center, is made with gentle curving lines in contrast to the flat, hexagonal base plate, which is supported by *neko-ashi* ("cat's legs"). The blue-green patina, resulting from its having been buried in the earth, is considered to enhance the beauty of this piece.

梅竹文透釣灯籠

Openwork Hanging Lantern with Plum-Bamboo Motif
Cast Bronze
Height: 31 cm.
Muromachi Period
Important Cultural Property
Owned by: Tokyo National Museum

138

139

52

DURING THE Kamakura Period, a priest named Eisai introduced tea to Japan from China. This led to the development of the tea-ceremony and consequently to the manufacturing of tea kettles. Kettles specifically for use in the tea-ceremony were cast mainly in Ashiya (Fukuoka Prefecture) and Sano Temmyo (Tochigi Prefecture). The two centers also produced Buddhist bells, pots, and ordinary kettles. The kettles cast at these places were called *Ashiya-gama* and *Temmyo-gama* respectively.

Ashiya-gama were cast from the mid-Kamakura Period through the Muromachi Period, but later declined in popularity. The characteristics of this type were the smooth finish and decorative casting of the body.

The shape of this kettle is called *shinnari-gama* (literally, "truth-shaped kettle") and it is thought to have had a brim on the lower part of the body.

On the front of the kettle is a tranquil scene of deer under the outspread branches of a maple tree. In sharp contrast to this repose, three rushing stags are dynamically rendered on the back. The ground, with the exception of the patterned portions, is in *arare*, a pattern of dots in relief. The fixtures for loops on both sides are fashioned in the form of ancient *kimen* (ogre masks). The cover is in *arare* and the knob is shaped like a *torii* (archway of a shrine), suggesting the Kasuga Shrine in Nara which is famous for its deer.

This piece was made in the early part of the Muromachi Period, but there are no damaged parts and all the designs are clearly legible.

140

楓
群
鹿
図
釜

Kettle with Deer Under Maple Tree Design
Cast Iron
Diameter of Body: 26.4 cm.
Muromachi Period
Important Cultural Property
Owned by: Mr. Ryo Hosomi, Osaka

53

THIS KETTLE is a *Temmyo-gama*, cast at Sano Temmyo, Tochigi Prefecture, where kettles for ordinary household use were cast as early as the Heian Period.

Kettles were cast in Japan from the Nara Period and records indicate that large kettles were offered to prominent temples. These were similar in casting technique to the *chanoyu-gama* made specifically for use in the tea-ceremony from the late Kamakura Period on.

In contrast to the *Ashiya-gama*, the Temmyo-gama rarely has any decorative designs. It is characterized by peculiar shapes and an effort to bring out the textural quality of the cast iron. Most of the Temmyo kettles are done in cast iron with *oarare* (rough dotted relief) and *arahada* (rough surface) texture.

This type of tea kettle, called *semehimo-gama*, has loops placed right beside the mouth. The surface of the kettle shows faint signs of hand lathe finishing.

責紐釜

Semehimo Tea Kettle
Cast Iron
Diameter of Body: 26.2 cm.
Muromachi Period
Owned by: Mr. Takiji Takano, Aichi Prefecture

142

54

THE cloisonné technique had been introduced to Japan as early as the Tumulus Period, and can be seen in objects preserved in the Shosoin. It subsequently fell into disuse, but rose to popularity again during the Momoyama Period. The brilliant color and gold of this type of art suited the flamboyant taste of this period and was extensively employed on architectural fittings, such a *hikite* (catch handles), *kugikakushi* (ornaments for hiding nailheads) and on sword ornaments.

The *kugikakushi* shown—plum flower, daffodil, and paulownia crests—coated with cloisonné enamelling and gilded, are typical of this type of fitting, and are in perfect harmony with the brash architecture and rich screen paintings of the same period. The shape of the metal *hikigane*, or handle, on the lower right-hand piece also exhibits outstanding workmanship.

七宝金具

Shippo or Cloisonné Metal Fittings
Momoyama Period
Owned by: Mr. Ryo Hosomi, Osaka

55

A SET consisting of a *kogai* (bodkin fitted on one side of the sword sheath), *menuki* (rivet bead), and *kozuka* (small dagger fitted on the other side of the sword sheath) is called *mitokoromono*. The manufacturing of these pieces belonged to the category of chasing work, which had a separate development from that of sword guard making. *Kogai* and *menuki* are seen on swords of the Kamakura Period, but GOTO Yujo is known to be the first craftsman specializing in this field. The art became hereditary in the Goto family and the Goto orthodox school flourished from the Muromachi through the Edo Periods.

GOTO Joshin was the third generation master of this family. The design of the set shown here, depicting a monkey reaching out to grab the moon reflected in the water, was a popular one during the latter part of the Muromachi Period. The engravings are done on a red bronze ground covered with *nanako* with gold inlay work. The *kogai* and *menuki* were made by Joshin, but the *kozuka* was by his successor. A small inscription, "Goto," is seen on the back of the *kogai*.

猿猴捕月図三所物

Mitokoromono (Sword Accessory Set) with Monkey Reaching for Moon Design
Made by: GOTO Joshin
Kogai: length: 22.5 cm., width: 1.2 cm.
Menuki: length: 4 cm., width: 1.5 cm.
Kozuka: length: 9.5 cm., width: 1.3 cm.
Muromachi Period
Important Cultural Property
Owned by: Mr. Moritatsu Hosokawa, Tokyo

146

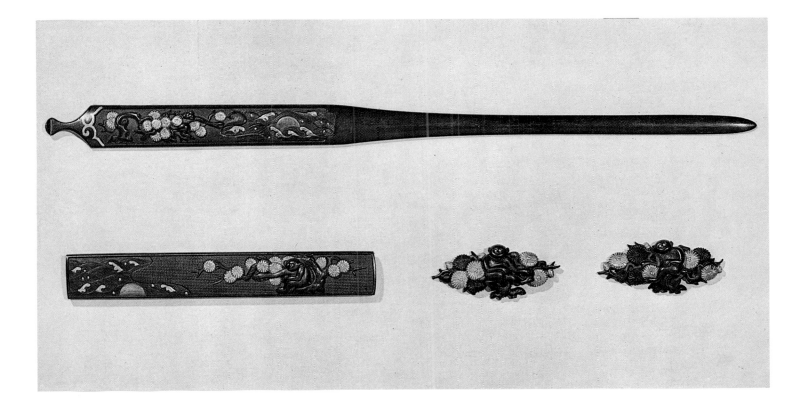

春日野鐔　花雲七宝鐔　鶴丸透鐔

56

Tsuba (Sword Guards)

SWORD GUARDS were originally made for the practical purpose of protection. Iron sword guards can be found on straight swords of the Tumulus Period and were in evidence up to the end of the Edo Period, though with variations in shape, style, and workmanship.

The *kara-tsuba* (Chinese sword guard) was popularly used for decorative swords in the Nara and Heian Periods. For combat swords, round or oblong iron sword guards or guards wrapped in leather were used up to the Muromachi Period.

Sword guards were made by swordsmiths and armor makers as a sideline in the earlier periods. After the Muromachi Period, however, we find a class of craftsmen specializing exclusively in swords, and occasionally, other metal accessories. These craftsmen did a good business until the early Meiji Period when it was prohibited to wear swords.

1) KANEIE I is famous as the originator of pictorial decorations on guards and this piece is celebrated as one of his masterpieces. On the iron ground of the round-cornered guard an autumn scene of the Kasuga plains of Nara is depicted in relief (in a technique called *sukidashi-takabori*, in which the ground is carved away to bring out the pattern in mezzo relief), and silver inlay work. The use of copper inlay on the *torii* arch adds variety to the colored metal work.

The back of the guard is also done in relief, depicting a maple tree.

1)　Kasugano Sword Guard
Made by:　Kaneie of Joshu Fushimi
Muromachi Period
Important Cultural Property
Owned by:　Mr. Moritatsu Hosokawa, Tokyo

2) THE TECHNIQUE of enamelling, seen in the Tumulus Period but in evident decline since, was revived by HIRATA Dojin in the Momoyama Period.

This guard is said to be the work of Dojin. It is of iron, round in shape, and decorated with enamel inlay and openwork. Flower and cloud designs are inlayed in colorful enamel. The perforations are moon-shaped and hat-shaped on four sides.

2)　Sword Guard Decorated with Flower and Cloud
Designs in Enamel
Reputedly made by:　HIRATA Dojin
Momoyama Period
Important Cultural Property
Owned by:　Mr. Tadanao Yoshii, Osaka

3) TSUCHIYA Yasuchika was one of the *Nara-ha Sansaku*, the three great metal work artists of the Nara school, specializing in sword mountings and accessories during the middle of the Edo Period.

The guard with a rounded crane design done in openwork on bronze is representative of his elegant work.

3)　Sword Guard with Circled Crane Design in
Openwork
Made by:　TSUCHIYA Yasuchika (Tou)
Edo Period
Owned by:　Mr. Tomijiro Miyazaki, Kanagawa
Prefecture

148

漆芸

Lacquer Ware

57

LACQUER is a product indigenous to Japan, China, Korea, Vietnam, Thailand, and other Asian countries, but it is not known exactly when it was first put to use. Lacquer wares excavated from mounds in southern China, the oldest in the world, were made in the period from 403 B.C. to 221 B.C., but the techniques were by then already considerably advanced. The oldest lacquer relic found in Japan is from the late Jomon Period.

New lacquer techniques were introduced to Japan in connection with Buddhism in the sixth century, and there was significant development during the eighth century, influenced by the high technical level of Chinese lacquer work in the T'ang Dynasty. This is apparent from the various treasures now in the Shosoin, which were made during the Nara Period.

This jewel-belt box, which was used to store leather belts decorated with jewels, is made of wood, coated with lacquer, and has inlays of thin gold sheets, *raden*, and crystals. *Raden*, a technique introduced from China for inlaying mother-of-pearl patterns, was also applied to bare sandalwood and other wooden materials.

Karahana (Chinese flower) designs, a large flower in the center and eight encircling smaller ones, are rendered on the cover. The sides have designs of floral petals, clouds, and flying birds in *raden*. The inside of the box is covered with brocade.

Delicate leaf veins engraved on the inlaid shells and coloring applied beneath the inlaid crystals are characteristic of the workmanship of this period.

螺鈿玉帯箱

Jewel-Belt Box in Raden
Diameter: 25.6 cm.
Height: 8.75 cm.
Nara Period
Preserved in: Shosoin Repository, Nara

152

58

MAKI-E, as the name implies, is a picture made by spraying powdered gold: the desired pattern is painted with lacquer and powdered gold is sprayed over it. The word *maki-e* first appears in the classic, *Taketori Mono-gatari*, written in the ninth century. The *maki-e* technique, however, was used in an earlier period, and a lacquered sword sheath done in gold and silver *maki-e* is preserved in the Shosoin. This is the only extant *maki-e* art object of the Nara Period. Another gold and silver painting method, using a mixture of gold or silver powder and glue, was widely practiced during that period. The method, in effect, resembles *maki-e*, but the latter became dominant because of its durability and the relative freedom of expression it permitted.

The cover of this sutra box is executed in the technique called *togidashi maki-e* (covered with additional coats of lacquer, rubbed with a charcoal stick, and polished) on a *heijin* lacquered ground with sparsely scattered gold dust. The Kurikara Dragon and a sword at the center symbolize the deity Acala (Fudo-myoo); Cetaka and Kimkara, two urchin attendants, stand on the rocks surrounded by waves. Around the three figures are falling lotus petals. The clever brush work and distribution of gold and silver powders clearly indicate the high degree of development in *maki-e* art during the Fujiwara Period. It is believed that the box was originally three-tiered, the middle tier having been lost. Gilt bronze lotus shaped fittings for loops are attached to the sides.

倶利伽羅龍蒔絵経箱

Sutra Box with Kurikara Dragon Design in Maki-e
Length: 31.2 cm.
Width: 19 cm.
Height: 5.8 cm.
Fujiwara Period
National Treasure
Owned by: Okunoin, Taimadera Monastery, Nara

154

59

THE LACQUER arts of the Fujiwara Period, along with all the other arts, showed a distinct departure from Chinese influence in both design and workmanship. This was largely due to the emergence of a purely Japanese style of life centered around the aristocracy. Rooms were elaborately furnished with chests, incense burners, shelves, inkstone boxes, dressers, mirror boxes, cosmetic kits, etc., arrangements being changed according to the season. The use of lacquer ware was greatly expanded, black lacquered objects rendered in *maki-e* being especially popular.

This box, which was used as a container for combs, powder case, and other cosmetic aids, is one of the few extant pieces from that period.

On a lacquered background with sparsely scattered gold dust (*heijin*), flying sparrows have been executed in the *togidashi maki-e* technique. On the inner sides of the box, plum branches are depicted in silver *maki-e*.

The wings of the sparrows, and the grass are rendered in a delicate mixture of gold and silver dust, called *aokin*, which is typical of the period.

野辺雀蒔絵手箱

"Handy" Box with Designs of Sparrows in the Fields
*   in Maki-e*
(*Detail in Actual Size*)
Length: 28.5 cm.
Width: 42 cm.
Height: 18.5 cm.
Fujiwara Period
Important Cultural Property
Owned by: Kongoji Monastery, Osaka

156

60

IN THE Fujiwara Period lacquer ware became more distinctively Japanese. The designs, for instance, tended toward more simplified, natural expression, pictorial representation of nature being most common. All the Fujiwara arts exhibit this tendency, but none so prominently as the *maki-e* designs.

On the top and sides of this chest, there is a scene of plovers at play among irises and water plantain, done in *maki-e* and *raden*. Instead of the conventional gold and silver dust, gold and *aokin* dust is used in the *maki-e*, the effect being accentuated by the combined use of the *raden* technique.

The chest is said to have contained altar objects connected with esoteric Buddhism.

158

沢千鳥蒔絵螺鈿小唐櫃

Small Chest with Design of Plovers in Marsh
in Maki-e and Raden
Length: 31 cm.
Width: 40.2 cm.
Height: 29.7 cm.
Fujiwara Period
National Treasure
Owned by: Kongobuji Temple, Wakayama Prefecture

61

IN GENERAL, the lacquer work of the Kamakura Period inherited the style of the previous Fujiwara Period. But the shapes and designs became stronger and sharper. Contours, which had been soft and elegant, now became tense. The covers of Kamakura caskets, for example, are quite abruptly curved at the edges. The sense of swelling, too, became more pronounced.

The pictorial representations lost some of the tenderness of the preceding period as more graphically realistic drawing gained in popularity. This development is also noticeable in the paintings of the period.

The lyrical scene on the cover and sides of this casket marks it as a transitional piece. The execution combines a number of different techniques, the principal one being the *togidashi maki-e*, which is combined with the *raden*, used to represent the bush-clover blossoms and birds. The rocks and the backs of the deer are executed primarily in *nashiji* (tiny bits of cut gold foil sprinkled over the lacquered ground so as to achieve an aventurine-like surface). Thus, a striking variety of color and tone is achieved.

The metal fittings for the loops are engraved with bush-clover blossom patterns in relief. Autumn plants and birds in flight are rendered in *togidashi maki-e* on the inside of the cover and in an inner compartment.

秋野蒔絵手箱

"Handy" Box with Autumn Field Design in Maki-e
Length: 22.5 cm.
Width: 29.7 cm.
Height: 16.1 cm.
Kamakura Period
National Treasure
Owned by: Izumo Taisha Shrine, Shimane Prefecture

160

62

THIS INKSTONE box is a product of the early Kamakura Period. The cover has chrysanthemum and fence designs in *raden* on a gold *maki-e* ground. The inside of the cover has a similar motif done in *togidashi maki-e* on an aventurine lacquer ground.

The box contains an inkstone in the center, and a gilt silver water container with a chased chrysanthemum design. There are compartments on each side, which have designs similar to those on the inside of the cover.

It is to be noted that gold is used for the *maki-e* instead of a combination of gold and silver or gold and *aokin* as was common in the Fujiwara Period.

Of all the pieces composing a Japanese writing set, it is on the box that the best workmanship has always been lavished, while in China, the inkstone was the primary object of attention.

籠菊螺鈿蒔絵硯箱

*Inkstone Box with Chrysanthemum and Fence Design in
    Maki-e and Mother-of-Pearl Inlay*
Length: 26 cm.
Width: 24 cm.
Height: 5.5 cm.
Kamakura Period
National Treasure
*Owned by: Tsurugaoka Hachiman Shrine, Kamakura,
      Kanagawa Prefecture*

162

163

63

ON THE cover and all four sides of this box, butterflies and peony arabesques are rendered on an aventurine (*nashiji*) ground. The flowers and butterflies are inlaid with mother-of-pearl (*raden*) and thin silver sheets; the details of the butterflies are engraved and then filled with gold, while those of the flowers are done in gold *maki-e*, such inlaying of thin cut metal sheets on a lacquered surface is called *hyomon*. It was introduced from China during the Nara Period, fell into disuse in the Fujiwara Period, and was revived in the Kamakura Period, when it was often combined with *maki-e* techniques. Metal fittings done in relief are attached for the loops on the sides of the box. The inside of the cover and compartments in the box are of the same pattern done in *togidashi maki-e* on an aventurine ground.

This type of box ordinarily contained cosmetics and usually had two compartments, one small and one large. A mirror box was placed at the bottom and other items, such as powder case, incense box, tooth-black box, plate to mix rouge, comb, rouge brush, scissors, tweezers, were all neatly arranged. Combs, brushes, tweezers, etc. were usually wrapped in beautifully designed folding paper cases. The contents of this particular box have been lost, except for one compartment.

蝶螺鈿蒔絵手箱

*"Handy" Box with Butterfly Design in Maki-e and
    Mother-of-Pearl Inlay*
Length: 25.2 cm.
Width: 35.2 cm.
Height: 21.0 cm.
Kamakura Period
National Treasure
Owned by: Mr. Kazukiyo Hatakeyama, Tokyo

164

64

RADEN, originally introduced from T'ang China, was thoroughly nationalized by the end of the Fujiwara Period. The practice of using it jointly with *maki-e* contributed to its vogue, and a very high level of workmanship was attained in the Kamakura Period. Chinese literature mentions that the *raden* technique was developed in Japan, and it should be noted that lacquer desks and saddles in *raden* were exported to China and Korea.

Highly advanced techniques of *raden* are manifest in this saddle. On a black lacquered ground cherry branches and blossoms are inlaid with mother-of-pearl, executed in the *raden* technique, giving it the aspect of a painting. The workmanship, involving the cutting of fragile shells into intricate forms and inlaying them on the curved surface, is especially noteworthy.

The brilliance and sparkle of such saddles apparently suited the taste of the military leaders of the Kamakura Period, when individual combat was more common than the collective warfare of later periods.

桜螺鈿鞍

Saddle Decorated with Cherry Blossom Design in Mother-of-Pearl Inlay
Height of front arch: 30.6 cm.
Height of back arch: 32.5 cm.
Kamakura Period
Important Cultural Property
Owned by: Mr. Nagatake Asano, Kanagawa Prefecture

166

167

65

THE MAKI-E workmanship of the Muromachi Period is imbued with a spirit of deep tranquility, perhaps due to the influence of Zen Buddhism.

The designs on this small writing table at first glance seem rather flamboyant. But a closer look reveals that the proportions and the colors are actually quite refined.

Tables like this one were often used at poetry parties, the poem sheets being placed on them. In post-Muromachi times the table would make a set with an inkstone box— an indispensable item in the trousseau of a bride of the *samurai* class.

168

菊蒔絵文台

Writing Table with Chrysanthemums in Maki-e
Length: 32.4 cm.
Width: 46.2 cm.
Height: 9.7 cm.
Muromachi Period
Owned by: Suntory Art Museum, Tokyo

Inside of Cover

66

DURING the Heian Period the technique of *togidashi maki-e*, the application of an additional coat of lacquer over the original *maki-e*, which was then rubbed with charcoal sticks to obtain burnished effects, was very popular. In the following Kamakura Period, *taka maki-e* (relief *maki-e*), which was made by applying gold *maki-e* over thick coats of a mixture of coarse yellow ochre and raw lacquer to achieve a relief effect, was developed. In the Muromachi Period, these two techniques were frequently combined, as in this inkstone box.

The design on the outside of the cover depicts a "great drum" used in *gagaku* (court music) in *taka maki-e* and inlaid gold sheets; the inside of the cover represents a scene of Mt. Saga, Kyoto, in delicate *togidashi maki-e* and gold inlay. Thus, the two designs on the cover are of completely unrelated subjects, which was characteristic of the period.

Also typical is the *uta-e* (literally, "poem-picture") on the inside of the cover. Several key words of a *waka* (31-syllable poem), suggesting the scene of Mt. Saga, are inscribed in decorative cursive characters within the picture space.

This combination of the plastic and literary arts is another feature of the Muromachi Period.

嵯峨山蒔絵硯箱

Inkstone Box with View of Mt. Saga in Maki-e
Length: 27.3 cm.
Width: 23.9 cm.
Height: 5.4 cm.
Muromachi Period
Owned by: Nezu Art Museum, Tokyo

170

67

THE SHOGUN ASHIKAGA Yoshimasa (1435–1490) was a confirmed aesthete who took a deep interest in the arts. His example and patronage had a stimulating effect on the arts of the Higashiyama Period (so-called because of the residence of Yoshimasa at Higashiyama in Kyoto), during which many *maki-e* masterpieces were produced.

This inkstone box is said to be one of the five which Yoshimasa especially favored.

On the square face of the box-cover, a night scene is rendered on a *nashiji* (aventurine lacquer) ground. The moon is a sheet of silver; the hillside is done in *togidashi maki-e;* the deer, rock, flowers, and grass are depicted in relief. The reverse of the cover shows a man in his hut listening to a distant deer. The theme of this scene is taken from a well-known *waka* in the *Kokinshu,* which describes the autumn solitude of a mountain village, where the poet was awakened one night by the sounds of deer.

The two compartments within the box are decorated with designs of Japanese pampas grass and arrowroot in *maki-e.*

172

春日山蒔絵硯箱

Inkstone Box with View of Mt. Kasuga in Maki-e
Length: 23.9 cm.
Width: 22 cm.
Height: 4.9 cm.
Muromachi Period
Important Cultural Property
Owned by: Nezu Art Museum, Tokyo

68

INSCRIPTIONS on the base of this brilliant red lacquer bowl show that it was made in 1391 A.D. and was used at a Buddhist temple. It is hand lathe finished, and the profile of the bowl bears a slight resemblance to the Tenmoku bowls of Sung China.

This bowl, the tray shown on the jacket, as well as other utensils of this period, finished in red lacquer over an under-coating of black lacquer, are popularly referred to as *negoro-nuri* wares. The red lacquer finish becomes worn with use, revealing the black underneath, an accidental effect which contributes greatly to the beauty of these pieces. The name derives from the red lacquer utensils for daily use made by priests of the Negoro Temple from the latter part of the thirteenth century through the sixteenth century. There are very few extant pieces actually made at the Negoro Temple.

朱漆塗椀

Red Lacquered Bowl
Diameter: 11.4 cm.
Height: 6.8 cm.
Muromachi Period
Owned by: Tokyo National Museum

174

69

THE DESIGN of autumn plants on this pot is rhythmic, natural, and in complete harmony with the shape of the vessel. The design is typical of the so-called *kodaiji maki-e* (see next plate): the naturalistic rendering of the plants as they are actually seen in the field achieves an unusually rhythmical decorative effect. Autumn plants, as seen in *yamato-e* screen paintings and in other *maki-e* of earlier periods, are usually used in conjunction with deer, the moon, etc., to establish a seasonal atmosphere. In this case, however, they are used as the major subject of the decorative design.

The ingeniously hinged cover which can be partly opened, and the handle which moves freely up and down show that the artist was concerned, not only with the decorative, but also with the functional aspects of the design.

薄葛蒔絵湯桶

Pot with Japanese Pampas Grass and Arrowroot
  Designs in Maki-e
Height: 28.5 cm.
Diameter: 2.2 cm.
Momoyama Period
Owned by: Mr. Gonroku Matsuda, Tokyo

176

70

IN THE Momoyama Period, lacquer craft moved into a new stage of development, especially with regard to the utilization of *maki-e*. The delicate and complex designs of the previous period gave way to bright, gorgeous representations. Simpler but forceful techniques came to be used.

What is usually called *kodaiji maki-e* best represents the lacquer ware of this period. The name derives from the Kodaiji monastery in Kyoto, built by Kodai-in, widow of TOYOTOMI Hideyoshi, which has various furnishings, utensils, and decorations in the same style *maki-e*; many of these objects are said to have been used by Hideyoshi and his wife.

This reading stand has chrysanthemum, pampas grass, and other autumn plant designs rendered in simple, naturalistic, yet decorative *maki-e*. Into this natural setting, large paulownia crests are boldly injected, creating an effective contrast in design.

秋草蒔絵見台

Reading Stand with Autumn Flowers in Maki-e
Height: 57 cm.
Length of stand: 29.2 cm.
Width of stand: 37.5 cm.
Momoyama Period
Owned by: Tokyo National Museum

178

71

JAPAN first encountered the West in 1543, when some Portuguese were stranded on a small island off southern Japan, and Western Christian culture greatly influenced the Japanese during the following hundred years. In 1641, however, the Tokugawa Shogunate adopted a policy of seclusion, whereafter contact with the West was limited to Dutch traders at Nagasaki.

The lacquer ware of that age did not escape foreign influences. The designs of imported items were freely imitated, and backgammon boards and cabinets with *maki-e* decorations, for example, were made for export.

This box contained a short sword given to a powerful lord in northern Japan by TOYOTOMI Hideyoshi.

The inner box is of black lacquer, with paulownia crests in relief *maki-e* on the outside and wild chrysanthemum designs in silver *maki-e* on an aventurine ground decorating the entire inner surface. The outer box is done in gold *maki-e* with chrysanthemums in diaper patterns, resembling certain Western textile designs.

180

蒔絵二重短刀箱

Double Short Sword Boxes with Maki-e Decorations
Outer Box Length: 47.6 cm.
             Width: 11.7 cm.
            Height: 13.3 cm.
Inner Box Length: 44.9 cm.
             Width: 8.8 cm.
            Height: 8.4 cm.
Momoyama Period
Important Cultural Property
Owned by: Mrs. Mako Homma, Yamagata
                Prefecture

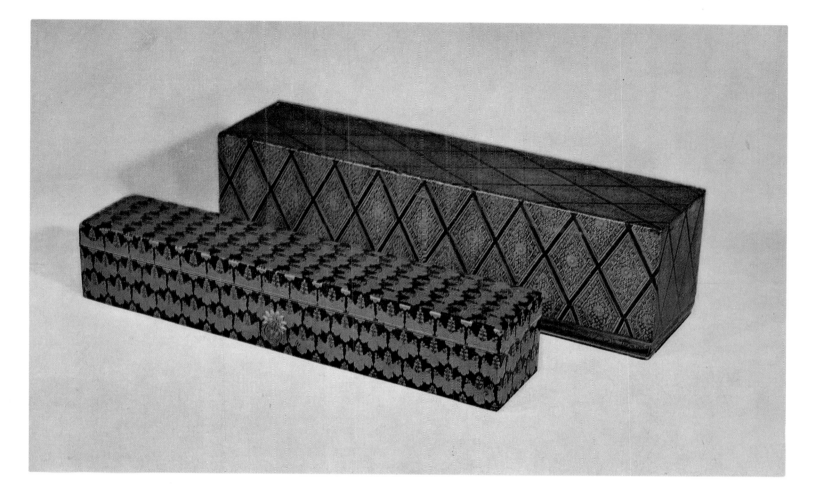

72

THE TECHNIQUE of *raden* (inlaid mother-of-pearl), first imported from T'ang China, reached a high level in the Kamakura Period, only to fall into disuse in the Muromachi. *Raden* techniques of Ming China were newly introduced in post-Muromachi times, and were followed, in the late sixteenth century, by the *wari-gai* (cracked shell) process, introduced from Yi Dynasty Korea.

These bright red lacquered bowls are done in this *wari-gai* technique, petals of cherry blossoms being rendered in cracked shells.

The bowls were reputedly designed by ODA Urakusai, a younger brother of ODA Nobunaga, who dominated the country briefly in the late sixteenth century. Urakusai was a celebrated master of the tea-ceremony, and the founder of the Uraku-ryu school of tea. And certainly the refined taste of the *chajin* (tea cultists) is evident in the design and execution of these bowls. The large bowl on the front left was used for rice and the one on the right for soup. The two bowls in the background were for serving hot and cold food, respectively.

The *zen*, or small individual dining table with indented corners, has four legs. The brims and legs are done in red lacquer. The face of the table is in black lacquer decorated with arabesque-style peonies in *raden*. The influence of Korean patterns is unmistakable in the arabesque.

明
月
椀

明
月
膳

Meigetsu Bowls
Diameter: rice bowl 14.1 cm.
*   soup bowl 13.1 cm.*
*   flat bowl 13.7 cm.*
*   deep bowl 11.2 cm.*
Momoyama Period
Owned by: Meigetsuin Monastery, Kanagawa
*   Prefecture*

Meigetsu Zen (individual dining stand)
Length & Width: 32 cm.
Height: 8 cm.
Momoyama Period
Owned by: Meigetsuin Monastery, Kanagawa
*   Prefecture*

182

183

73

AT THE beginning of the Edo Period, two styles of lacquer ware were common: the development of the technically rather simple *kodaiji maki-e* of the Momoyama Period, and a further elaboration of the lavish *togidashi maki-e* and *taka maki-e* of the Muromachi Period.

Noteworthy examples of the latter style are the so-called *hatsune maki-e* pieces preserved by the Tokugawa Reimei-kai. The name *hatsune* (literally, "first sound") derives from the name of a chapter in the *Genji Monogatari*. They have depicted on them scenes, of palaces and gardens with ponds, of the Fujiwara Period, in *togidashi maki-e*, inlay of cut-gold sheet, chased metal, and carved corals.

This shelf, called the *zushi-dana*, is one of the three, which, with numerous other accessories, constitutes a marriage set used by the ruling Tokugawa family. The tenth generation head of the Koami family, Nagashige (1599-1651), spent three years in making this set. The Tokugawa *Aoi* crest is seen on each of the pieces.

KOAMI Michinaga, the founder of this lacquer artisan family, served ASHIKAGA Yoshimasa in the late Muromachi Period, and his descendants the Tokugawa Shogunate.

初音蒔絵棚

Ornamental Shelf—One of the Hatsune Set of Lacquered Furniture
Length: top shelf   100.4 cm.
*   lower shelf   85 cm.*
Width: 39.4 cm.
Height: 78.4 cm.
Early Edo Period
Owned by: Tokugawa Reimei-kai, Tokyo

184

74

THE OLDEST lacquer ware we now have are some bowls of the Jomon Period excavated in Aomori Prefecture. These were small, coated with black lacquer outside and red lacquer inside. Later, during the tenth century, a particular shape for lacquered bowls for food was established, and there has been no radical change since, as there has also not been any considerable change in the mechanics of eating (way of holding the bowls, method of using chopsticks, etc.); but from the late Muromachi Period there were certain innovations, different types of bowls being made for different kinds of foods, as in the case of the Meigetsu Bowls. There were simple floral designs on lacquered bowls from the Kamakura Period, and later *raden* was employed.

These bowls, called *Hidehira-wan, Nambu-wan,* or *Hojoji-wan,* have simple patterns done in colored lacquer and thin cut-gold sheets; the inside of the bowl is red lacquer. The name derives from FUJIWARA Hidehira, a powerful lord in northeastern Japan, during the twelfth century, who built the Chusonji monastery in Hiraizumi. However, these bowls only date from the sixteenth century.

There are also similar lacquered bowls called *Ouchi-wan,* named after OUCHI Yoshitaka, a military lord who ruled on the southern tip of Honshu about the same time.

秀衡椀

Hidehira Bowls
Diameter: 12.5 cm.
Height: 11.2 cm.
Edo Period
Owned by: *Tokyo National Museum*

186

75

THE USE of red, yellow, and green lacquer to paint pictorial designs on lacquer ware was practiced in China as early as the fourth century B.C. Colored lacquer was also used quite early in Japan, but not to the same extent. This method developed rapidly during the Momoyama Period, influenced by the taste for brilliant luxurious objects, as well as the popularity of colorful screen and *fusuma* (sliding door) paintings. The importation of Chinese lacquer wares with oil color decorations might also have served as a stimulus.

During the Edo Period, due to the comparative simplicity of the method, *urushi-e* (lacquer painting) rose to sudden popularity, especially in the provinces.

Inside this sturdy, eminently usable tray, whose shape shows some Chinese influence, grapes are rendered in yellow, green, and black lacquer on a red ground. Bamboo leaves and birds decorate the black lacquered brim, the leaves being lacquered in red and green.

The birds are done with a kind of oil pigment called *mitsuda-e*.

葡萄漆絵盆

Tray with Grape Designs in Colored Lacquer
Diameter: 39.6 cm.
Height: 7.8 cm.
Edo Period
Owned by: Tokyo National Museum

188

76

IN THE early Edo Period, *maki-e* designs were further refined and reached their peak in the hands of HON'AMI Koetsu (1558-1637). Koetsu excelled in painting, calligraphy, and ceramics; and his talents are also apparent in *maki-e*. It is not known whether he made the *maki-e* himself, but it is quite certain that he did create the designs and supervise the work.

The design of this box derives from a *waka* (31-syllable poem) contained in the *Gosenwakashu*, a collection of poems edited on Imperial order in 951 A.D.

The surface of the cover is lacquered and heavily sprinkled with gold dust. Waves and pontoons are depicted on this ground and a bridge spans the design. The *waka*, except for the characters for "boat" and "bridge" (which are represented in the design), are written in inlay of thick silver plate. The striking design and the unprecedented way of using different materials are illustrative of Koetsu's bold, creative genius.

190

舟橋蒔絵硯箱

Inkstone Box with Bridge Design in Maki-e
Designed by: Koetsu
Length: 24.2 cm.
Width: 22.8 cm.
Height: 11.8 cm.
Edo Period
Owned by: Tokyo National Museum

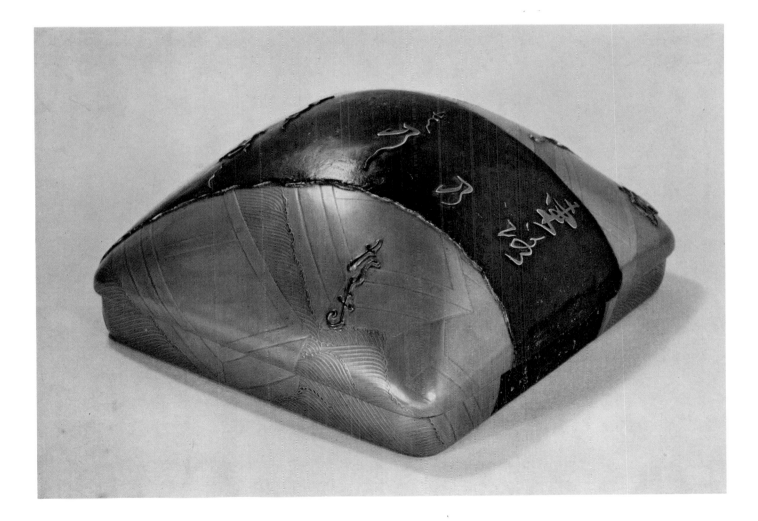

77

THE PREFERENCE for elaborate ornamental workmanship and sumptuous decorations (see Pl. 74) eventually led to the gaudy ornamentation and extravagant use of costly materials, which are characteristic of the Genroku era (1688-1703). This taste for luxury was largely due to the long peace and to the prosperity of the merchant class.

The simple but fresh workmanship of the previous period was completely submerged by gaudy designs in *maki-e*, which were not justified by any compensating technical advances. There were, however, a few creative artisans, and OGATA Korin (1658–1716) was the most outstanding among them. Korin followed in the steps of HON'AMI Koetsu and finally created his own style of workmanship.

The upper compartment of this double-decked inkstone box was used for the inkstone and the lower compartment for paper. The cover is made so that it is easily removable.

The *yatsuhashi* (eight bridges) design is suggested by a chapter in the *Ise Monogatari*. Lead is used for the bridge, silver for the stakes, shells for the iris flowers, and the stems and leaves are rendered in *maki-e*. The skillful use of various materials and the ingenius composition of the design are unparalleled in the history of this art.

八橋蒔絵硯箱

Inkstone Box with Yatsuhashi Design
By: Korin
Length: 27.4 cm.
Width: 19.7 cm.
Height: 14.2 cm.
Edo Period
Important Cultural Property
Owned by: Tokyo National Museum

192

193

78

THIS PIECE of furniture serves both as a screen and as a shelf. The flowing water-plantain design decorating the three small drawers and the top of the shelf suggest the influence of the decorative style of Korin. It is in simple *maki-e*, but the effective use of color, the design of the furniture itself, as well as the workmanship, all give an impression of freshness and a certain elegance, in sharp contrast to the contemporaneous trend toward over-decoration.

On the back, gold foil is pasted. The round windows, covered with white gauze, are translucent. Bars of transparent and colored glass are inserted in both ends of the shelf.

194

水草蒔絵飾棚

Ornamental Shelf with Water Plantain Design in Maki-e
Length: 15.5 cm.
Width: 76.2 cm.
Height: 48.3 cm.
Edo Period
Owned by: Tokyo National Museum

79

THIS BLACK lacquered square *zen*, or individual eating stand, is one of a set of five. On it is depicted a pleasant riverside scene, with running water, water-drops on bush-clover, water plantain, and two little water fowls. A touch of red lacquer coloring on the grass provides an accent to the comparatively plain gold *maki-e* design. The geometrical angularity of the running water contrasts sharply with the freely drawn lines of the other objects.

The other pieces of the set have designs of grape vines, wisteria, butterflies, birds, and other natural objects.

沢潟漆絵膳

Zen with Water Plantain Design in Maki-e
Length: 29.2 cm.
Width: 29.2 cm.
Height: 7.4 cm.
Edo Period
Owned by: Tokyo National Museum

80

MITSUDA-E is a type of oil painting applied on lacquer, using pigments mixed with perilla oil and *mitsuda-so* (lead oxide) as a dessicative. This technique was imported from China during the Nara Period, as is evident from the decorative work on a sword scabbard preserved in the Shosoin Repository. It was not, however, seen again in Japan until the Momoyama Period, when it was once more introduced.

The brim of this square tray is painted with olive-green lacquer, and its face with dark red. On the face is a painting of a Chinese lady holding a flower basket, done in *mitsuda-e*.

Full advantage is taken of the *mitsuda-e* technique, in which various subtle coloring effects, as in the woman's drapery, are easily obtainable, though they would have been impossible with colored lacquer.

唐人物密陀絵膳

Zen with Chinese Figure Design in Mitsuda-e
Length: 32.5 cm.
Width: 32.6 cm.
Height: 2.3 cm.
Edo Period
Owned by: Tokyo National Museum

198

鳴　群　芦
蟬　馬　雁
蒔　蒔　蒔
絵　絵　絵
印　印　印
籠　籠　籠

81

Inro

INRO, as the name implies, were originally small receptacles for containing a seal and small red ink pad, which were imported into Japan from China during the Muromachi Period. The *inro* of that time were rather large in size and were hung as ornamental pieces in the house. They were later made smaller and were used as portable medicine containers hung from the *obi*, or sash. This new use encouraged the development of the art of *inro*-making, as well as the carving of *netsuke* (a small sculpture, generally of wood or ivory, tied at the end of the cord on which the *inro* was hung, and serving the purpose of a stopper and ornamental piece).

With the increased popularity of carrying *inro*, even such famed artisans as OGATA Korin began to make designs for them. Also, craftsmen specializing in *inro*-making were hired by the Shogunate and feudal lords.

KANSAI was a well-known *maki-e* artist employed by the ruling Tokugawa family. This piece is made of bamboo, and a cicada is depicted in *maki-e* on the bamboo texture.

Inro with Cicada Design in Maki-e
By: KOMA *Kansai (1767–1835)*

YAMADA JOGA lived in Edo (Tokyo) and became an official craftsman attached to the Tokugawa Shogunate, for which, according to one document, he was making *inro* in 1683. He specialized in *inro* and incense box making. This piece depicts a herd of horses in gold and silver *maki-e*.

Inro with Design of Herd of Horses in Maki-e
By: YAMADA *Joga*

IIZUKA TOYO was employed as the official *inro*-maker for a feudal lord on Shikoku in the mid-eighteenth century. The design of this *inro* looks as if it had been drawn in black ink, but actually it is a *togidashi maki-e* using a mixture of charcoal dust and silver to depict the rush and wild geese on a ground of densely sprinkled gold dust. The darkest black was obtained by using charcoal dust made from camellia trees. The different shades of black are made by mixing an appropriate amount of silver dust.

Inro with Rush and Wild Geese Design in Maki-e
By: IIZUKA *Toyo*

200

染織

Textiles

82

THIS IS a part of a banner made of *ra*, or thin silk gauze. It is a fabric of extremely complicated weave, apparently accomplished by twisting into the warp a set of four threads, instead of the usual two. This particular method of weaving had been developed in China during the Han Dynasty, but it was introduced into Japan only in the seventh century. The conventional design in this weave consisted of diamond patterns, since the technique makes it relatively easy to weave diagonal straight lines. The piece illustrated here is unusual in its arabesque-like designs.

The flower-shaped pattern was dyed by the *kyokechi*, or clamped-stencil, technique. The details of the method are not clearly understood, but it would seem that the material was folded two or four times, clamped between two thin boards in which the design was cut, and then the dye solution poured on it. The line running across the upper part of the material is where it was folded, and the designs on either side of this line form a symmetrical pattern. The question arises as to how it was dyed in so many colors. One would guess that, as in woodblock printing, each color to be printed on the material was applied to a different set of boards, but this is mere speculation since the technique was completely lost during the following Jogan and Fujiwara Periods. Undoubtedly the clamped-stencil dyeing technique, too, must have been brought over from China, but it was widely used in Japan during this period.

花文纐纈羅幡

Ra Silk Banner with Flower Design (*detail*)
Nara Period
Owned by: Tokyo National Museum

204

205

83

THE HORYUJI, built in Nara in the seventh century, is one of the oldest temples in Japan. It is a veritable monument of the Asuka Period, preserving all kinds of objects related to the regency of Prince Shotoku. At the beginning of the Meiji Period, most of the treasures connected with the Prince were presented to the Imperial Household and are today housed in the Tokyo National Museum.

One item in the collection, the piece illustrated here, is part of a banner, the *kanto ban*, which was perhaps hung from a canopy during Buddhist ceremonies. The origin of the word *kanto* is obscure; it seems to derive from a foreign name, the place where such an ikat weave must have originated, and it is likely that this banner was imported, perhaps from as far away as Indonesia, India, or Iran.

Several banners are stored in both the Horyuji and the Shosoin. Yet the *kanto ban* is the most valuable in that it is the longest and retains the original pattern in the best condition. It is woven of silk in plain weave, and the designs are rendered by the different colored dyes on the warp. The pattern of curved lines is thought by some experts to represent human figures.

広東幡

Kanto Ban or Banner (detail)
Sixth or Seventh Century
Important Cultural Property
Owned by: Tokyo National Museum

206

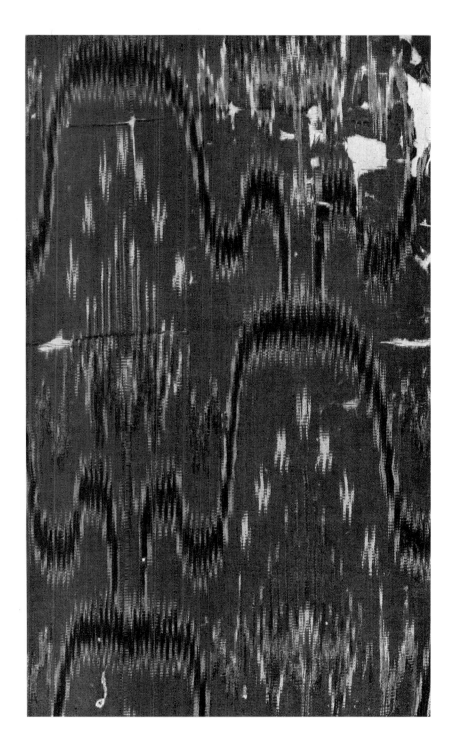

84

SHU-CHIANG brocade, produced in Shu-chiang Province, now Szechwan, in China, became famous during the third century for its beautiful red color. This piece of compound weaving was called "Shu-chiang brocade," apparently because of its color. Several pieces of similar weave are preserved in the Shosoin, all of which were presumably brought over to Japan from China.

China exerted a great influence, both directly and indirectly, by way of Korea, upon Japan's weaving art in its early stages. The fragment here, for instance, one of the oldest extant pieces, might easily have been used as a model by Japanese artisans of the Nara Period. The same may be said of the piece in Plate 83, which is the reason we have illustrated these two fabrics.

It is made by a technique called *tate nishiki*, whereby the pattern is woven with a multi-colored warp (in this case three colors are used). *Tate nishiki*, used in China during the Han Dynasty, is believed to be the oldest method of compound weaving. It was perhaps during the late seventh or early eighth century that the technique of *yoko nishiki* brocade weaving, with patterns rendered by colored threads in the woof, was introduced to Japan. The fact that most of the pieces of *nishiki* preserved in the Shosoin are *yoko nishiki* supports this assumption.

This fragment is part of a sash which belonged to Princess Kashiwade, the consort of Prince Shotoku.

蜀江錦下帯

"Shu-chiang Brocade" Sash of Compound Weave (detail)
Sixth or Seventh Century
Important Cultural Property
Preserved in: Tokyo National Museum

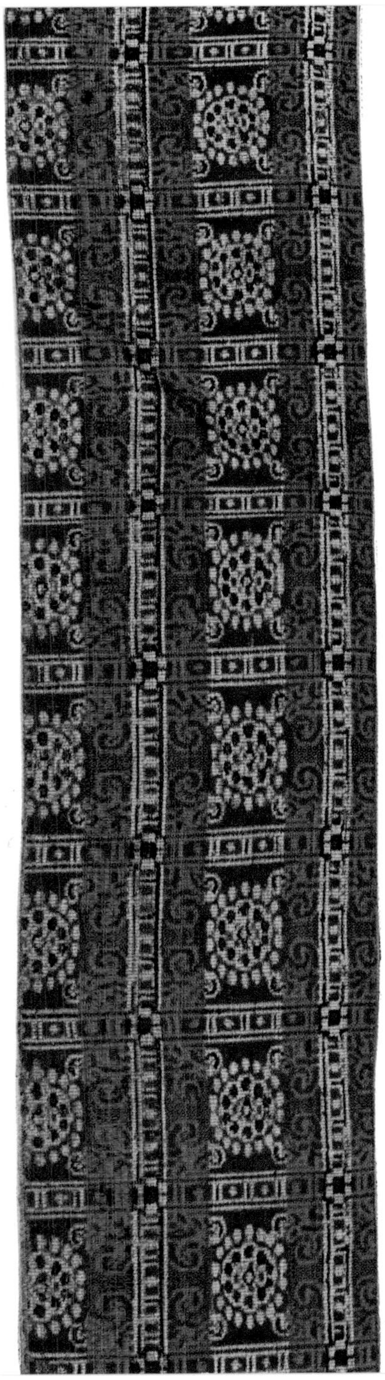

85

THE KUMANO Hayatama Grand Shrine of Shingu City, Wakayama Prefecture, owns a large number of national treasures and important cultural properties.

According to the shrine records, this piece is a sacred robe dedicated by the *shogun* ASHIKAGA Yoshimitsu to the shrine, toward the end of the fourteenth century. The shape as well as the design of the garment, however, are typical of the style popular among court ladies of the later Fujiwara Period. Many layers of such robes were worn on top of a white undergarment and a long trailing crimson *hakama* (pleated skirt). The characteristics of the garments of the Fujiwara Period are the absence of dyed designs, and the extensive use of woven patterns. This trend was inevitably accompanied by a decline in the three dyeing techniques of the Nara Period, namely, *kyokechi* (stencil dyeing), *rokechi* (wax resist dyeing), and *kokechi* (the tie-and-dye technique). The former two were lost during the period between the tenth and thirteenth centuries.

This garment is made of *aya* (twill weave) silk, in which the geometrical design of leaves and flowers is woven by means of brocaded wefts. On this ground is a circular design called *fusenryo*, brocaded in yellow, white, and purple.

青色小葵地に浮線綾文袿

Uchiki, Twill Weave with Brocaded Design
Muromachi Period
National Treasure
Owned by: Kumano Hayatama Grand Shrine,
Wakayama Prefecture

210

86

THE PIECE illustrated here is the upper part of the *yoroi-hitatare* (under-armor garment) allegedly worn by Prince Morinaga, who was killed in 1335. The design, composed of crab-shaped peonies and butterflies, is woven in a regularized pattern on a red ground.

That only a military leader was permitted in those days to wear a *yoroi-hitatare* made of *nishiki* (compound weave) suggest the value that was attached to this fabric. The *samurai* used the *yoroi-hitatare*, not only to indicate his rank, but also to enhance his personal dignty; in those days, as later, the military man was anxious to wear the most gorgeous garments possible on the battlefield to crown with glory what might, after all, be the last moments of his life.

However, this piece actually compares rather poorly with similar works of earlier periods, the designs being fairly monotonous and the workmanship inferior. This would seem to be the result of a deterioration of the arts of weaving and dyeing brought about by the many years of rule by practical military men.

赤地錦蟹牡丹模様鎧直垂

*Under-Armor Garment of Nishiki with Peony and
    Butterfly Designs on Red Ground*
Kamakura Period
Owned by: Tokyo National Museum

212

87

THIS COAT belonged to UESUGI Kenshin (died in 1578), a *samurai* famous as a wise and brave leader in the civil wars of the sixteenth century. The *dobuku* is said to be a rudimentary form of today's haori (a kind of light half-coat).

Splashed over a red ground of silk material are designs of snow-covered willows, peonies, and stylized paulownia leaves done in embroidery. Such colorful garments were popular among the military men of that age and reflect their extravagant life.

The embroidery is freely and effectively used to create naturalistic effects which are impossible in woven designs. However, the design is not pictorial, as it becomes in later periods, and the symmetrical and regular arrangement of motifs covering the entire garment still retains the conventions of woven design.

紅地雪持柳模様胴服

*Dobuku, with Snow-Covered Willow Designs on
    Red Ground*
Late Muromachi Period
Owned by: Uesugi Shrine, Yamagata Prefecture

214

88

THIS DOBUKU, worn by UESUGI Kenshin, is made of various fabrics patched together. In ancient times, when clothing material was scarce, it was a widespread practice among the common people to patch small pieces of fabric together to make their clothes. Also Buddhist priests were, at one time, supposed to make their *kesa* (or surplice) out of cast-away rags or fragments of material donated by the faithful. (Today the *kesa* is still made of several pieces of material, symbolic of the original practice.) Furthermore, it was the custom for a man who had reached the age of sixty to be presented with a *kimono* made up of different pieces of material, each given by a friend with good wishes for health and longevity. The obvious design potentialities of the patchwork technique were utilized in many ways, such as, for example, the *katami gawari* (see Pl. 98) in which each half of the *kimono* is of different color or design.

This *dobuku* is made of extremely expensive and rare materials imported from China during the sixteenth century; altogether seventeen different kinds of fabric were used.

織物縫合せ胴服

Coat with Patches of Different Fabrics
Late Muromachi Period
Important Cultural Property
Owned by: Uesugi Shrine, Yamagata Prefecture

216

89

THE DOBUKU, in this plate, believed to have been a gift from TOYOTOMI Hideyoshi to a feudal lord, utilized the *tsujigahana* dyeing technique, which was popular during the Muromachi and Momoyama Periods. It was a tie-and-dye method, in which the outline of the design was stitched with thread, this portion then being firmly tied and dyed.

Although the design appears to be rather simple, it actually required an unusually high level of workmanship to execute a colorful design such as this solely by the *tsujigahana* method. Even today, nearly four centuries after it was made, the skilled rendering of the design can be seen in the sewing and tying of every single stitch: the white horizontal line in the lower part, for instance, has the precision of a line drawn with a ruler. Each paulownia crest, dyed in a different color—yellow, green, purple, and light blue—appears to have been tied and soaked in its respective color-dye solution separately. It is remarkable that not the slightest trace of the running of color is detectable.

桐紋散らしに矢襖模様胴服

Dobuku with Paulownia Crest and Scattered Arrow Designs
Momoyama Period
Important Cultural Property
Owned by: Mrs. Takako Akashi, Kyoto

218

90

A GREAT change took place in the Japanese apparel industry between the fifteenth and sixteenth centuries. People developed a simpler taste in clothing in the austere atmosphere following the civil wars, and it was during this period that the court-lady's costume consisting of many layers was discarded in favor of the *kosode* (see note to Pl. 92) or what is today called the *kimono*.

This simplification in clothing style led to changes in design, and greatly accelerated the development of colorful pictorial patterns. The period marks a transition in preference in Japanese clothing material from woven to hand-dyed designs. However, since the emphasis during the preceding several centuries had been almost exclusively on woven designs, the only remaining non-weaving design method was the tie-and-dye technique, which was put to maximum use in this period and was gradually elaborated by combination with other techniques, ultimately resulting in the development of the so-called *tsujigahana* style (see Pl. 92 and 93).

This *tsumugi* cloth (made of uneven hand-spun silk) must have been part of a *kosode*. The designs were outlined in small stitches over thick threads, which were tightly pressed and dyed.

紬地藤に葵模様辻が花裂

Tsumugi Cloth Dyed in Tsujigahana Style, with
*   Wisteria and Aoi Design*
Muromachi or Momoyama Period
Owned by: Mr. Kihachi Tabata, Kyoto

220

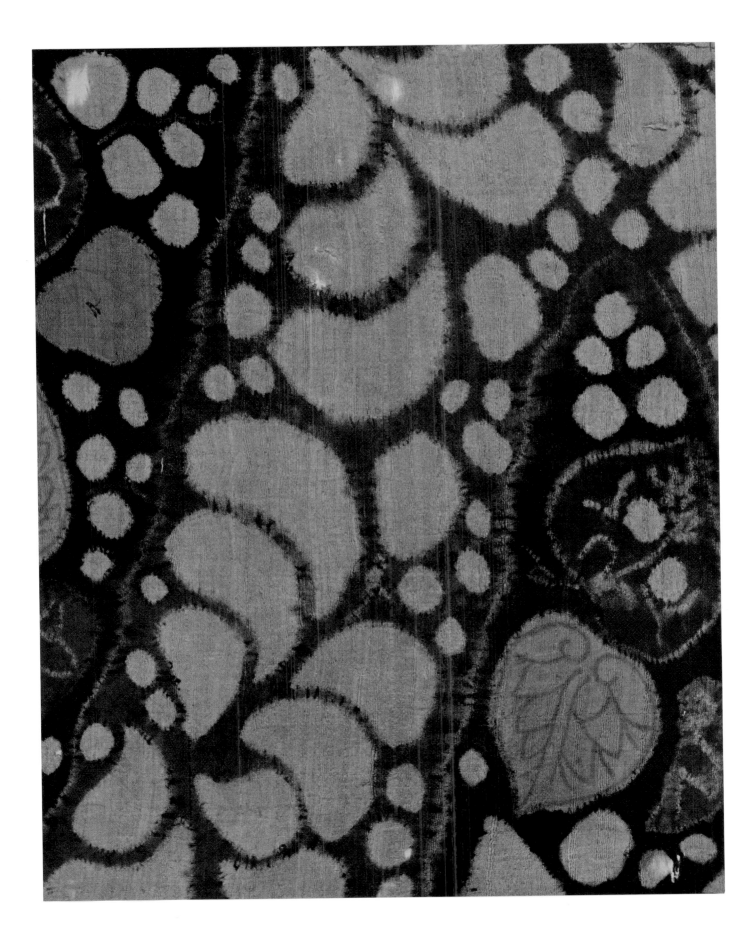

221

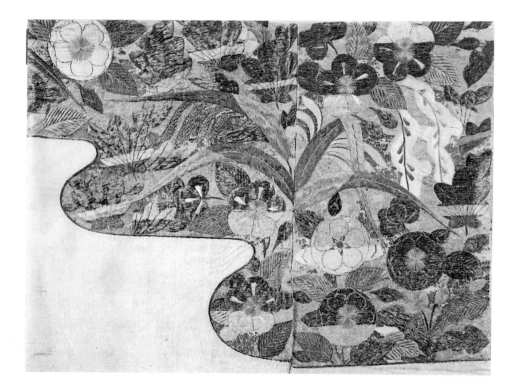

Detail

91

DESIGNS splashed across the shoulder and the lower portion of the garment (*kata-suso-moyo*) were popular from the fifteenth to the mid-sixteenth century. The designs, as in this costume, were rigidly confined to a limited area, in contrast to those of a later period, which were freely distributed over the whole costume.

Nuihaku (embroidery and gold-leaf *applique*) became more widely used during this period. Embroidered designs had the advantage of being freer, less restricted by the technical limitations of woven designs. But the very ease of the technique often led to its lavish over-use for the mere display of technical skill.

The embroidery of the Momoyama Period, however, usually avoids the ostentatious abuse of skill, being tastefully employed to add color and beauty to the design.

This *Noh* costume of the late sixteenth century was used when playing child roles. On a gold leaf background are scattered embroidered flowers of all seasons. The shape of the sleeve, typical of the style of this time, is extremely narrow in relation to the width of the costume.

白地草花模様肩裾縫箔

Kosode with Flower Design in Nuihaku on a White Ground
Momoyama Period
Owned by: Tokyo National Museum

222

223

92

ACCORDING to the dedicatory legend on the lining of this *kosode*, it was a dancing costume presented to some Shinto shrine in 1566, to be worn in the ritual dance celebrating the New Year.

The *kosode* (literally "small-sleeved") was originally a form of plain undergarment for court ladies in the Heian Period, layers of colorful clothing with long trailing sleeves being worn over it. As a result of the civil wars and the emergence of the *samurai* class, simple and abbreviated forms of clothing became popular. The small-sleeved undergarment of the court ladies was transformed into an outerwear, covered with appropriate designs. The simple clothing of the common people also began to bear colored patterns and to be closer in style to the *kosode*. Thus, the *kosode*, which is so called because of the small opening of the sleeve and not with reference to the actual size of the sleeve itself, can be said to be the original form of the present-day Japanese *kimono*.

In the historical development of the *tsujigahana* dyeing technique, this piece stands chronologically midway between that shown in Plate 90 and the one in Plate 93. The early method consisted, in the main, of a rather coarse tie-and-dye technique, reinforced by hand-outlining or applied gold leaf. To meet the rising demand for more delicate designs, the use of hand-painting and hand-outlining techniques was increased. Later, embroidery too was introduced. The workmanship of this *kosode* represents the *tsujigahana* dyeing technique at the mid-point of its development.

花鳥模様辻が花小袖

Kosode with Tsujigahana Flower and Bird Design
Muromachi Period
Important Cultural Property
Owned by: Tokyo National Museum

224

93

THIS KOSODE is believed to have belonged to TOKUGAWA
Ieyasu (died 1616), founder of the Tokugawa Shogunate.

The upper shoulder part is dyed purple, by the tie-
and-dye technique, in a shape popularly known as a
matsukawabishi (triple diamond) pattern. The Tokugawa
aoi family crest, done in the same technique, appears in
five places in the purple portion. In the lower part, a
large bamboo design emerges from the upper left hand
corner, curving in a graceful line down toward the lower
right. The tie-and-dye work in the bamboo stalk is ex-
ceedingly fine. From this stalk emerge young shoots dyed
in pale blue-green, again in tie-and-dye. The hand-outlining of the edges of the leaves and stalk in India ink is
effective in adding clarity to the forms. This method is
frequently employed in the *kimono* of the period in order
to offset the haziness of the design that is likely to result
from the tie-and-dye technique.

The *kimono* in this plate clearly illustrates the transformation from regular geometric designs, necessitated by
weaving techniques, to the free naturalistic designs which
were possible by dyeing.

The *tsujigahana* method reached its peak towards the
end of the sixteenth century, soon after which it fell
into sudden eclipse, the tie-and-dye and hand-outlining
techniques, of which *tsujigahana* was composed, thence
following separate courses of development.

松皮菱に竹模様辻が花小袖

Kosode with Tsujigahana Triple-Diamond Shape and
    Bamboo Design
Momoyama or Early Edo Period
Owned by: Mr. Shinzo Noguchi, Tokyo

226

94

THIS COSTUME is of *rinzu* material (satin damask) in which large oxalis crests are deftly introduced by the use of the tie-and-dye technique and embroidery. The method is much the same as sixteenth century *tsujigahana* dyeing, but the effect is entirely different, chiefly because of the highly restrained use of the tie-and-dye method. This subdued tie-and-dye technique prevailed throughout the late seventeenth and early eighteenth centuries, the vogue lasting until the *yuzen* hand-dyed design came to dominate Japan's textile art.

Apparently a product of the late seventeenth century, this article illustrates the transition from an even distribution of the design over the entire *kimono*, typical of the sixteenth century, to an irregular concentration. The influence of ink painting is increasingly apparent in the use of plain backgrounds, the effectiveness of which can be judged from the present example.

The design consists only of large oxalis crests. Family crests were derived from a great variety of objects, abstracted and stylized, many developing out of textile designs (though the converse was also often true).

赤地丸に酢漿草紋小袖

*Kosode with Circled Oxalis Crest Pattern on Red
  Ground*
Early Edo Period
Owned by: Mr. Kihachi Tabata, Kyoto

95

RED, black, and purplish-gray blocks, rendered by the tie-and-dye method, stand out against a white background. The so-called snow-ring pattern, stylized suggestions of snow softly piled up on leaves and branches, covers half the middle section and the shoulder part, giving the effect of a coat draped over the shoulders. Such arrangements are common in *kimono* of the late seventeenth and early eighteenth centuries.

A distinctive feature of the design of this and of some later *kimono* is the effect achieved by the horizontal division that separates the design at waist level. This was to accommodate the prevailing trend toward wider *obi*.

In the bamboo design near the lower portion, the tie-and-dye method applied to the bamboo stalks is reinforced by embroidery, in which all the leaves are rendered, adding further color variety. That the balanced effect thus achieved was carefully calculated, is indicated by the fact that the space for the leaves was left undyed to enhance the effectiveness of the embroidery.

With the perfection of the *yuzen* technique in the following period, embroidery came to play a subsidiary role, used only as a means of enhancing and highlighting the hand-dyed design.

230

白地松竹に雪輪首抜模様小袖

Kosode with Pine-Bamboo and Snow-Ring Design on White Ground.
Early Edo Period
Owned by: Mr. Kihachi Tabata, Kyoto

233

97

THIS NOH costume, which is believed to date from the late sixteenth or early seventeenth century, was used for feminine roles. Forceful *tatewaku*, or flowing vertical lines, are appliqued in gold leaf on a brown ground. The process of applying gold leaf begins with the tracing of paper patterns with glue. This is followed by the application of gold leaf while the glue is still wet; as the glue dries, the gold leaf settles in place.

The design consists of large lilies, embroidered in white and yellow, among which are distributed tiny noble court carriages. No longer scattered evenly over the entire *kimono* as in the preceding period, the patterns are freely and unsymmetrically arranged.

However, a trace of the evenly-patterned designs, characteristic of the preceding era, is still present: little space is left open without some sort of design surrounding the main motif. Kosode of the late seventeenth century make effective use of the contrast between the plain solid-color ground and the boldly patterned designs.

茶地百合に御所車模様縫箔

Noh Costume with Lily and Court Carriage Designs in
   Nuihaku on Brown Ground
Momoyama Period
Owned by: Tokyo National Museum

234

235

98

THE TWO halves of the *kimono* are of different materials, one being brocaded and the other a crimson satin. The designs are written characters from an anthology of poetry.

This *Noh* costume was used for male roles. It is believed to be a product of the mid-seventeenth century, because of its style and the calligraphic form of the characters used in the design. The design is free from the repetitiousness of pattern generally found in woven designs. Furthermore, the characters are cleverly arranged so that the decorative effect is shown to best advantage when the garment is worn. Each stroke of the characters is such a graceful line that one might be tempted to doubt whether the design had in fact really been woven. Gold thread had been in use for a long time in embroidery and *tsuzure* (tapestry weave) brocade, but it was not until the close of the sixteenth century, when Chinese gold brocade technique was introduced, that the entire ground was lavishly inter-woven with gold thread, as it was in the illustrated piece. The gold brocade was woven of gold threads made of finely cut gilded paper, which is flat, as opposed to the ordinary round thread used for weaving. This use of paper-backed gold foil requires the adroit use of a hooked bamboo stick in the process of weaving the threads into the fabric.

金紅詩歌模様片身替厚板

Noh Costume with Poems Brocaded on a Gold and Crimson Ground
Edo Period
Owned by: Tokyo National Museum

236

99

THIS NOH costume was used in portraying male characters of noble birth. Herons and reeds are profusely scattered over the whole of the *kariginu* (literally, "hunting suit") against a purplish-gray satin background. Herons, whose graceful silhouettes, accentuated by their long neck-lines and snowy white feathers are usually associated with femininity, here add a touch of delicate elegance to this male Noh costume.

Judging from the embroidery workmanship and the arrangement of designs strewn over the entire garment, it is estimated that this piece dates from the latter half of the sixteenth century. It is remarkable that the design does not seem overcrowded, despite the fact that practically every inch of space is filled with flying herons, no two of which are the same, though a close look reveals that the herons are arranged at regular intervals, all flying in the same direction.

No designs appear in one area on the back where a narrow sash is believed to have been tied when the garment was actually worn.

238

納戸地鷺模様狩衣

Noh Costume, Kariginu with Heron Design on
*   Purplish-Gray Ground*
Momoyama Period
Owned by: Hakusan Shrine, Gifu Prefecture

100

SHOWN HERE is a *kabuki* costume. *Kabuki* flourished during the Edo Period as a popular theatrical art, but was subject to stringent restrictions imposed by the Shogunate. For instance, there was a regulation against realistic impersonation of high-ranking *samurai* on the stage. This circumstance, however, encouraged the development of unique, often quite fanciful, *kabuki* costumes. The red one illustrated here is the dress for *Akahime*, or "red princess," one of the costumes used by *kabuki* actors when playing the role of a noble princess.

This *kimono* was worn by a *kabuki* actress who died at the close of the nineteenth century. Ordinarily, *kabuki* had an exclusively male cast, as it does today, but *kabuki* with a female cast was performed before the ladies of the feudal palaces, since the women's quarters were closed to men.

The level of workmanship in this costume is not too high, but after all, in a stage costume what is important is the effect from a distance. This *kimono*, which is not more than 100 years old, is nevertheless considered a valuable specimen, as old *kabuki* costumes are very rare.

240

赤地流水に桜模様振袖

*Furisode with Running Water and Cherry Blossom
   Design on a Red Silk Crepe Ground*
Edo Period
Owned by: Tokyo National Museum

101

THERE WAS generally more color in eighteenth century design than in that of the preceding century, but summer costumes tended to remain simple. Breezy ramie dyed in dark-blue was the usual material for summer *kimono*, though occasionally thin silk was used. *Kimono* material was supposed to vary with the social class of the wearer. For instance, common people wore cotton *yukata* dyed, in dark blue by the tie-and-dye technique or by stencil dyeing, while the *samurai* class favored the expensive ramie, elaborately designed in dark blue.

This summer *kimono* is perhaps the most extravagent from the Edo Period and represents the highest standard of workmanship. The exquisite design is one of the *tomegara*, or designs used exclusively for the close relatives of the Tokugawa Shogun.

A staggering amount of labor must have gone into the dyeing of this garment, for the whole ground, which had to be kept undyed, was covered with color resist paste, accounting for every detail of the design. The process may have taken as long as a year. Unlike *yuzen* dyeing, in which the colors are applied with brushes, this technique involves immersion in indigo solution at the risk of having the blue dye run into the white part. Such an extraordinarily elaborate method necessarily limited the number of *kimono* that could be made with it. This *chayatsuji* dye method was supposedly originated by CHAYA Sori during the Kan-ei era (1624-1644). It was used to dye formal clothing for women of the higher *samurai* class, and the Shogunate had a specialist in this type of dyeing in its employ.

This piece is believed to be a product of the mid-eighteenth century.

風景模様茶屋染帷子

Summer Kimono Dyed in Chayatsuji Style with
*   Landscape Design*
Middle Edo Period
Owned by: Nagao Art Museum, Kanagawa
*   Prefecture*

242

102

A JIMBAORI is a coat worn over armor on the battlefield, and is an integral part of a combat outfit, though there are both practical and ornamental types. The latter are characterized by their elaborate decoration, with which the wearer indicated his dignity, identified his rank, and, above all, perhaps embellished his final resting place. During the period of civil wars, both kinds of *jimbaori* were common, but once peace was restored, only the ornamental type continued to be made. The long era of peace in the Edo Period, from the seventeenth century through the first half of the nineteenth, encouraged the decorative development of the *jimbaori*, which was eventually transformed into a formal attire for outdoor use.

The piece illustrated here dates from around the middle of the eighteenth century and was presumably owned by a great feudal lord. It is made of imported woolen cloth, and sports a design of Dutch sailing ships. The design is rendered in an "inlay" technique, by which pieces of woolen cloth of different colors are set, level with the surface of the ground.

南蛮船模様陣羽織

Jimbaori or Over-Armor Garment with Dutch-Boat Design
Middle Edo Period
Owned by: Maeda Ikutoku-kai, Tokyo

244

103

JAPAN'S weaving and dyeing art developed spectacularly during the late seventeenth and early eighteenth centuries, with the perfection of the revolutionary dyeing technique called *yuzen*. The dyeing method of applying paste as a color resist, by means of a stencil, had long been in use. What made *yuzen* dyeing revolutionary was the high degree of freedom which this technique permitted in executing hand-dyed designs. The designs were finely outlined with a color resist made of rice paste, applied either with a paper funnel or a chopstick-like instrument. The outlined design was then filled in with the desired color or colors. No longer subject to the various technical limitations imposed by other traditional dyeing methods, such as the tie-and-dye technique, the ultimate in free pictorial *kimono* decoration was attained. However, this extreme freedom of selection of design and color often resulted in the mere gaudy elaboration of design or the gratuitous display of technical virtuosity.

A product of the mid-eighteenth century, the *furisode kimono* illustrated here features a stylized design of a sheaf of *noshi* (a ceremonial decoration used on gift packages, originally made of flattened, dried abalone). In the execution of the design, practically every technique in use in the Edo Period was utilized: *yuzen* dyeing, embroidery, the tie-and-dye technique, and gold-leaf *applique*.

The *furisode* is a *kimono* with long hanging sleeves (usually about 80 to 90 cm.) with the inner side of the sleeve left open.

246

熨斗模様振袖

Furisode Kimono with Noshi Design
Middle Edo Period
Owned by: Yuzen Seikai, Kyoto

104

IT WAS during the period from the latter half of the eighteenth century to the first decades of the nineteenth that the *yuzen* hand-dyed design achieved its fullest development, and narrative and symbolic designs began to become increasingly popular. Flower and bird patterns had to make way for such scenic themes as Japan's three famous landscapes or the eight scenic spots around Lake Biwa. Such designs often provided material for guessing games demanding a knowledge of what the designs stood for.

This *kosode* is one such example. Apparently made toward the end of the eighteenth century, it illustrates a scene in the Yoshiwara gay quarters of old Tokyo. A man with a child is riding in a palanquin, and at some distance from him is the main entrance gate of the Yoshiwara. The whole place is rendered in surprisingly minute detail: the inside of the *tatami*-matted rooms on the second floor is open to full view, and one can even distinguish the various kinds of food on the table.

吉原細見模様小袖

Kosode with Yoshiwara Gay Quarter Design
Late Edo Period
Owned by: Nagao Art Museum, Kanagawa
            Prefecture

248

105

KOMON, (literally, "small pattern"), like *chugata*, is a kind of stencil dyeing. Since the design cut in the stencil is extremely small, it cannot be traced with color resist from both sides of the material in the *chugata* fashion. Color resist, therefore, is for the most part applied to one side only; and in dyeing it is usual to apply the desired color or colors with a brush.

The difficult part of *komon* stencil dyeing is fitting each design into the other with no trace of awkward linking lines. A close look at the arabesques in this plate reveals that there is an overlapping of the patterns: where one pattern ends and another begins is not discernible unless one studies the stencil itself. Equally complicated is the task of making the stencil. For small designs, as many as 700 or 800 holes have to be punched on a stenciled one inch square. Such exacting work requires intricate instruments, which the artisan often makes himself. It takes an average of ten days to two weeks to complete one stencil for a *komon* design. A single unfortunate stroke towards the end—and the whole week's work is lost, and has to be begun all over again. This exacting technique is still kept alive by several outstanding artisans in the towns of Shiroko and Jike in Suzuka City, Mie Prefecture, who enjoy the protection of the government. *Komon* was popular among *samurai* for formal clothing during the Edo Period, but its origin is not clear.

小紋

Komon Stencil Dyeing
Edo Period

250

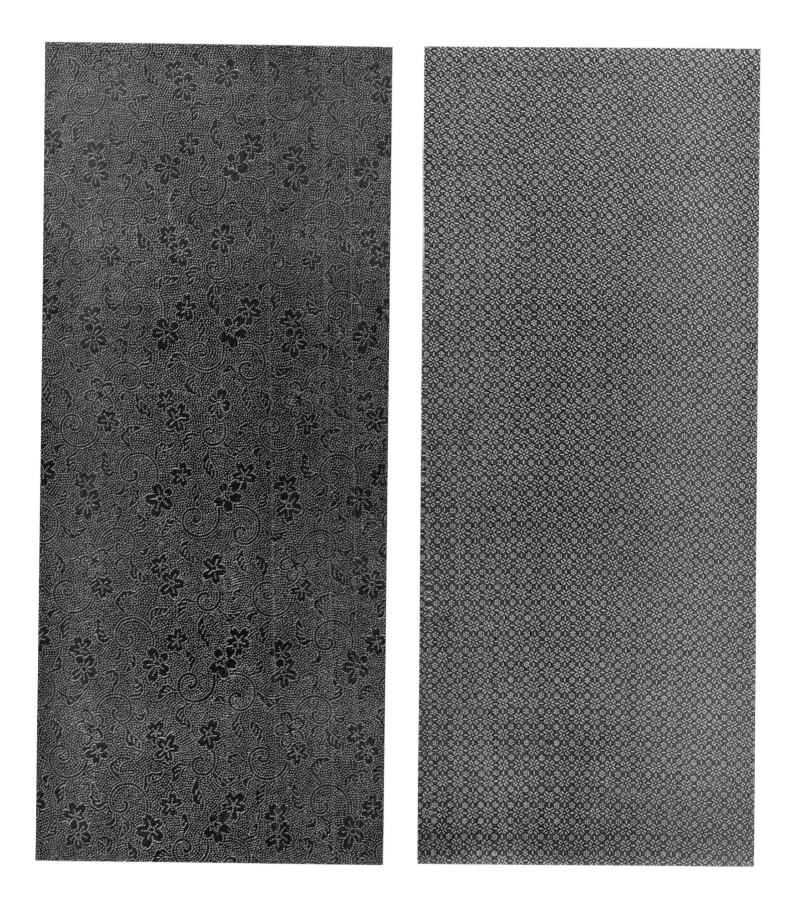

106

IN STENCIL dyeing, the medium-sized stencil is called *chugata*. However, the word ordinarily refers to the stencil used in dyeing cotton *yukata* materials.

When stencil dyeing first came into use, no one knows, but the relics of the garments worn by *samurai* in the sixteenth century are convincing evidence that the technique was already in use during that period.

The initial step in stencil dyeing is to stretch the cotton material on a piece of board some twenty feet in length. After the stencil, in which the desired design has been cut, is placed on the material, color resist paste is applied. These operations are repeated until the entire ground from end to end is covered. This unusually exacting method is required to ensure that the pattern comes out flawlessly, and that each design fits into the other with mathematical precision. When one side is thoroughly processed and dried, the already formed patterns are retraced very carefully with paste on the reverse side, so that the color will not run from either side when the cloth is soaked in indigo solution. After both sides of the cloth have dried, it is immersed in the dye. Later it is rinsed in running water until the color resist paste is removed.

The *yukata* material illustrated here was presumably made in the mid-nineteenth century.

中
型
模
様

Chugata Design
Edo Period

252

107

GENERALLY speaking, clothes of the common people are washed frequently and vigorously and thus wear out quickly. Moreover, the making of *kimono* is such that the materials when taken apart can be remade into a variety of things. For these reasons, there are very few old commoners' *kimono* remaining. Although the illustrated piece is no older than the nineteenth century, only fragments of it remain today.

During the Edo Period, the common people were subject to many petty laws regulating the details of their dress, and definitely discouraging them from elaborate indulgence. This led them to develop *kimono* unique in their own class and period, reflecting their taste for interesting designs and patterns, the like of which were not found in the *kimono* of the *samurai* class.

This *yukata* is believed to have been for use after bathing in summer. The selection of the old, battered umbrella as a motif, instead of just a plain one, is unusual. The rest of the design is composed of rain in diagonal lines and stylized rain dragons. The dragon is a mythical monster of Chinese origin and is believed to possess the power to bring rain.

破れ傘に雨龍模様浴衣裂

Yukata Material with Torn Umbrella and Rain Dragon Designs
Edo Period
Owned by: Mr. Tomoyuki Yamanobe, Tokyo

254

255

Chronology

There are numerous systems of chronology in use in works on Japanese history and art history. They are often at variance with each other and are not always consistently applied. The outline given here is designed to cover the historical references in the present volume only. It might be noted that the terms "Suiko" and "Asuka" are often used interchangeably and applied loosely to the whole era between the Tumulus and Hakuho Periods. Many works refer to the entire span between 645 and 793 as the Nara Period, sub-dividing it into the Hakuho and Tempyo Periods. Some authorities begin the Edo Period in 1603.

JOMON PERIOD
(–late 3rd century B.C.)

- Jomon earthenware developed in central and east Japan and gradually spread westward.

YAYOI PERIOD
(late 3rd century B.C.–late 3rd century A.D.)

- Introduction of rice cultivation.
- Introduction of metal culture.
- Production of Yayoi pottery, bronze mirrors, etc. started in Kyushu and spread eastward.
- *Dotaku* produced in the central part of Japan.

TUMULUS PERIOD
(late 3rd century–537)

- Monumental sepulchral mounds constructed to bury the chiefs of powerful clans; production of *haniwa* clay figures, Sue pottery started during this period.
- Textile craftsmen invited from China.

ASUKA PERIOD
(538-644)

    Suiko Period
    (538-644)

538

- Introduction of Buddhism.
- Architects brought over from China.
- Casting, chasing, wrought iron, metal inlay techniques advanced.

587

- Victory of Buddhist faction in the Imperial Court.

588

- A group of architects and craftsmen of Buddhist Art sent to the Imperial Court from Pekche.
- Reign of Empress Suiko (592–628).
  (Regency of Prince Shotoku 593–621)
- Large monasteries such as Horyuji, Hokoji, and Shitennoji constructed.

HAKUHO PERIOD
(645–709)

645

- Taika Reformation.

NARA PERIOD (710–793)	710	• The Imperial Palace moved to Nara. • The Todaiji monastery constructed. • Art treasures and other objects dedicated to the Great Buddha of the Todaiji monastery stored in the Shosoin Repository. • The *Manyoshu* poetry anthology compiled.

HEIAN PERIOD
(794–1184)
    Jogan Period
    (794–893)
    Fujiwara Period
    (894–1184)
	794
	
	894
	
	1053
		• The capital moved to Kyoto.
		• Tendai and Shingon Sects introduced.
		• Missions to T'ang China discontinued, providing opportunities for an indigenous style to emerge in the arts.
		• *Tale of Genji* by Lady Murasaki.
		• The elegant and elaborate taste of court officials greatly enhanced the advancement of the decorative arts of Japan.
		• Hoodo Temple of the Byodoin Monastery erected.
		• Many sumptuous temples built by the nobles.
		• *Maki-e* became extremely popular.

KAMAKURA PERIOD (1185–1333)	1185 1333	• The Taira clan overthrown and a military government established in Kamakura by Yoritomo of the Genji clan. • Development of metal work in connection with swords and armor greatly advanced. • Zen Buddhism introduced to Japan and became popular. • The six old kilns at Seto, Tokoname, Shigaraki, Tamba, Echizen, and Bizen. • The military government of Kamakura collapsed.
MUROMACHI PERIOD (1334–1572)	1338	• The Ashikaga family gained military control and established government headquarters in Kyoto. • Ashiya in Kyushu and Temmyo in Tochigi Prefecture became centers of kettle-making. • Specialists in making sword guards and other sword accessories, such as GOTO Yujo (1439–1512), established herditary families, contributing to the advancement of this art. • *Kosode*, the origin of the present day *kimono*, became the style of outer clothing. • ASHIKAGA Yoshimasa (1435–1490), the eighth Shogun, contributed greatly to the development of the arts by employing many artisans. • Priest Shuko reformed the tea-ceremony. • KOAMI Michinaga (1410–1478) first generation of the Koami family of *maki-e* artists.

(*Muromachi Period continued*)		· *Tsujigahara* dyeing method developed.
		· Beginning of cotton weaving.
	1543	· Portuguese sailors stranded at Tanegashima.
	1549	· Christianity introduced to Japan.
MOMOYAMA PERIOD (1573–1614)	1573	· ODA Nobunaga emerged victorious, subjugating most of the feudal lords.
	1583	· TOYOTOMI Hideyoshi succeeded Nobunaga and unified Japan.
		· SEN no Rikyu (1520–1591), a great tea-ceremony master.
		· Chojiro I (1516–1592), founder of the Raku kiln.
		· Production of Ming-style brocade, satin, satin-damask, *crepe-de-Chine* started.
		· *Kodaiji maki-e.*
		· Hideyoshi's expeditions to Korea.
		· Korean potters brought back to Japan by feudal lords after the expedition, and kilns started in Kyushu.
		· Karatsu kiln started by naturalized Koreans.
		· Mino kilns producing Ki-Seto, Shino, and Oribe ware flourished.
		· HON'AMI Koetsu (1558–1637).
	1603	· Tokugawa Shogunate established in Edo (Tokyo).
EDO PERIOD (1615–1867)	1615	· Fall of the Toyotomi family.
		· SAKAIDA Kakiemon (1590–1666).
		· Ko-Kutani porcelain and Imari porcelain flourished.
		· Pottery with enamel color by NONOMURA Ninsei (active in the second half of the seventeenth century).
		· *Chayatsuji* dyeing method developed.
		· *Yuzen* dyeing method developed.
		· OGATA Korin (1658–1716).
		· OGATA Kenzan (1663–1743).
		· Stencil dyeing (*komon* and *chugata*) developed.
MEIJI ERA (1868–1912)	1868	· Meiji Restoration.
TAISHO ERA (1912–1926)		
SHOWA ERA (1926–)		

List of Plates

T